The Kingfisher Book of

COMIC COMIC

V＊E＊R＊S＊E

Edited by Roger McGough
Drawings by Caroline Holden

Kingfisher Books

Kingfisher Books, Grisewood & Dempsey Ltd,
Elsley House, 24–30 Great Titchfield Street,
London W1P 7AD

First published in paperback in 1991 by Kingfisher Books
Originally published in hardback in 1986 by Kingfisher Books
10 9 8 7 6 5 4 3 2

BRITISH LIBRARY CATALOGUING IN PUBLICATION DATA
The Kingfisher book of comic verse.
1. Children's poetry in English, 1945- – Anthologies
I. McGough, Roger II. Holden, Caroline
821.9140809282

ISBN 0 86272 785 5

Research by Hilary Clough
Phototypeset by Waveney Typesetters, Norwich
Printed and bound in Great Britain by
BPCC Hazells Ltd
Member of BPCC Ltd

contents

some people never learn

faraway places

fair warnings

chew on this

hands, knees and bumps

meet the folks

tall stories

simply seasons

is anybbbody there?

all creatures great . . .

... and smallish

square pegs

LOOK OUT!

The witches mumble horrid chants,
You're scolded by five thousand aunts,
 A Martian pulls a fearsome face
 And hurls you into Outer Space,
You're tied in front of whistling trains,
A tomahawk has sliced your brains,
 The tigers snarl, the giants roar,
 You're sat on by a dinosaur.
In vain you're shouting 'Help' and 'Stop',
The walls are spinning like a top,
 The earth is melting in the sun
 And all the horror's just begun.
And, oh, the screams, the thumping hearts
That awful night before school starts.

Max Fatchen

WHATIF

Last night, while I lay thinking here,
Some Whatifs crawled inside my ear
And pranced and partied all night long
And sang their same old Whatif song:
Whatif I'm dumb in school?
Whatif they've closed the swimming pool?
Whatif I get beat up?
Whatif there's poison in my cup?
Whatif I start to cry?
Whatif I get sick and die?
Whatif I flunk that test?
Whatif green hair grows on my chest?
Whatif nobody likes me?
Whatif a bolt of lightning strikes me?
Whatif I don't grow taller?
Whatif my head starts getting smaller?
Whatif the fish won't bite?
Whatif the wind tears up my kite?
Whatif they start a war?
Whatif my parents get divorced?
Whatif the bus is late?
Whatif my teeth don't grow in straight?
Whatif I tear my pants?
Whatif I never learn to dance?
Everything seems swell, and then
The nighttime Whatifs strike again!

Shel Silverstein

DISTRACTED THE MOTHER SAID TO HER BOY

Distracted the mother said to her boy,
'Do you try to upset and perplex and annoy?
Now, give me four reasons – and don't play the fool –
Why you shouldn't get up and get ready for school.'

Her son replied slowly, 'Well, mother, you see,
I can't stand the teachers and they detest me;
And there isn't a boy or a girl in the place
That I like or, in turn, that delights in my face.'

'And I'll give you two reasons,' she said, 'why you ought
Get yourself off to school before you get caught;
Because, first, you are forty, and, next, you young fool,
It's your job to be there.
You're the head of the school.'

Gregory Harrison

THE MADNESS OF A HEADMISTRESS

Don't be a fool, don't go to school,
Don't put a foot outside –
Old Miss Oysterley
Is eating bubblegum,
Sellotape, tin-tacks and Tide!

Be like a mouse, stay in the house –
Her mouth is open wide –
Weird Miss Oysterley
Is drinking printer's ink,
Paint and insecticide!

Don't go near the Head, just stay in bed –
Jump in a box and hide –
Old Miss Oysterley
Is fond of the little ones –
Roasted or frittered or fried!

It's very sad, she's gone quite mad,
Her brain is quite petrified –
Poor Miss Oysterley
Munching through Infants I
That once was her joy and pride!

Gavin Ewart

SUPPLY TEACHER

Here is the rule for what to do
Whenever your teacher has the flu,
Or for some other reason takes to her bed
And a different teacher comes instead.

When this visiting teacher hangs up her hat,
Writes the date on the board, does this or that;
Always remember, you must say this:
'*Our* teacher never does that, Miss!'

When you want to change places or wander about,
Or feel like getting the guinea-pig out,
Never forget, the message is this:
'*Our* teacher always lets us, Miss!'

Then, when your teacher returns next day
And complains about the paint or clay,
Remember these words, you just say this:
'That *other* teacher told us to, Miss!'

Allan Ahlberg

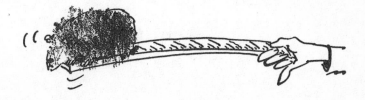

DOWN BY THE SCHOOL GATE

There goes the bell
it's half past three
and down by the school gate
you will see . . .

. . . ten mums in coats, talking
    nine babes in prams, squawking
    eight dads their cars parking
    seven dogs on leads barking

    six toddlers all squabbling
    five Grans on bikes wobbling
    four child-minders running
    three bus drivers sunning

    two teenagers dating
    one lollipop man waiting . . .

The school is out,
it's half past three
and the first to the school gate
. . . is me!

Wes Magee

READING SCHEME

Here is Peter. Here is Jane. They like fun.
Jane has a big doll. Peter has a ball.
Look, Jane, look! Look at the dog! See him run!

Here is Mummy. She has baked a bun.
Here is the milkman. He has come to call.
Here is Peter. Here is Jane. They like fun.

Go Peter! Go Jane! Come, milkman, come!
The milkman likes Mummy. She likes them all.
Look, Jane, look! Look at the dog! See him run!

Here are the curtains. They shut out the sun.
Let us peep! On tiptoe Jane! You are small!
Here is Peter. Here is Jane. They like fun.

I hear a car, Jane. The milkman looks glum.
Here is Daddy in his car. Daddy is tall.
Look, Jane, look! Look at the dog! See him run!

Daddy looks very cross. Has he a gun?
Up milkman! Up milkman! Over the wall!
Here is Peter. Here is Jane. They like fun.
Look, Jane, look! Look at the dog! See him run!

Wendy Cope

STREEMIN

im in the botom streme
wich means im not britgh

dont lik readin
cant hardly write

But all these divishns
arnt reelly fair

Look at the cemtery
no streemin there

Roger McGough

COLOUR OF MY DREAMS

I'm a really rotten reader
the worst in all the class,
the sort of rotten reader
that makes you want to laugh.

I'm last in all the readin' tests,
my score's not on the page
and when I read to teacher
she gets in such a rage.

She says I cannot form my words
she says I can't build up
and that I don't know phonics
– and don't know c-a-t from k-u-p.

They say that I'm dyxlectic
(that's a word they've just found out)
. . . but when I get some plasticine
    I know what that's about.

I make these scary monsters
I draw these secret lands
and get my hair all sticky
and paint on all me hands.

I make these super models,
I build these smashing towers
that reach up to the ceiling
– and take me hours and hours.

I paint these lovely pictures
in thick green drippy paint
that gets all on the carpet –
and makes the cleaners faint.

I build great magic forests
weave bushes out of string
and paint pink panderellos
and birds that really sing.

I play my world of real believe
I play it every day
and teachers stand and watch me
but don't know what to say.

They give me diagnostic tests,
they try out reading schemes,
but none of them will ever know
the colour of my dreams.

Peter Dixon

THE HERO

Slowly with bleeding nose and aching wrists
After tremendous use of feet and fists
He rises from the dusty schoolroom floor
And limps for solace to the girl next door
Boasting of kicks and punches, cheers and noise,
And far worse damage done to bigger boys.

Robert Graves

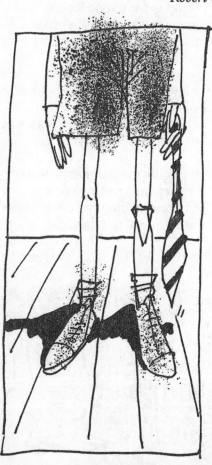

SHIRLEY SAID

Who wrote 'kick me' on my back?
Who put a spider in my mac?
Who's the one who pulls my hair?
Tries to trip me everywhere?
Who runs up to me and strikes me?
That boy there – I think he likes me.

Denis Doyle

OIC

I'm in a 10der mood today
   & feel poetic, 2;
4 fun I'll just – off a line
   & send it off 2 U.

I'm sorry you've been 6 o long;
   Don't B disconsol8;
But bear your ills with 42de,
   & they won't seem so gr8.

Anonymous

QUESTIONS

Do trains get tired of running
And woodworms tired of holes
Do tunnels tire of darkness
And stones of being so old?

Do shadows tire of sunshine
And puddles tire of rain?
And footballs tire of kicking
Does Peter tire of Jane?

Does water tire of spilling
And fires of being too hot
And smells get tired of smelling
And chickenpox – of spots?

I do not know the answers
I'll ask them all one day . . .
But I get tired of reading
And I've done enough today.

Peter Dixon

THE ANSWERS

'When did the world begin and how?'
I asked a lamb, a goat, a cow:

'What's it all about and why?'
I asked a hog as he went by:

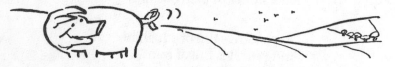

'Where will the whole thing end, and when?'
I asked a duck, a goose, a hen:

And I copied all the answers too,
A quack, a honk, an oink, a moo.

Robert Clairmont

PICKING TEAMS

When we pick teams in the playground,
Whatever the game might be,
There's always somebody left till last
And usually it's me.

I stand there looking hopeful
And tapping myself on the chest,
But the captains pick the others first,
Starting, of course, with the best.

Maybe if teams were sometimes picked
Starting with the worst,
Once in his life a boy like me
Could end up being first!

Allan Ahlberg

COME ON IN THE WATER'S LOVELY

Come on in the water's lovely
It isn't really cold at all
Of course you'll be quite safe up this end
If you hold tight to the wall.

Of course that fat boy there won't drown you
He's too busy drowning Gail.
Just imagine you're a tadpole.
I *know* you haven't got a tail.

Oh come on in the water's lovely
Warm and clear as anything
All the bottom tiles are squiggly
And your legs like wriggly string.

Come on in the water's lovely
It's no good freezing on the side
How do you know you're going to drown
Unless you've really tried.

What? You're really going to do it?
You'll jump in on the count of three?
Of course the chlorine doesn't blind you
Dive straight in and you'll soon see.

One – it isn't really deep at all.
Two – see just comes to my chin.
Three – oh there's the bell for closing time
And just as you jumped in!

Gareth Owen

TODAY IS VERY BORING

Today is very boring,
it's a very boring day,
there is nothing much to look at,
there is nothing much to say,
there's a peacock on my sneakers,
there's a penguin on my head,
there's a dormouse on my doorstep,
I am going back to bed.

Today is very boring,
it is boring through and through,
there is absolutely nothing
that I think I want to do,
I see giants riding rhinos,
and an ogre with a sword,
there's a dragon blowing smoke rings,
I am positively bored.

Today is very boring,
I can hardly help but yawn,
there's a flying saucer landing
in the middle of my lawn,
a volcano just erupted
less than half a mile away,
and I think I felt an earthquake,
it's a very boring day.

Jack Prelutsky

A POEM

a poem moves down a page

faster than a novel

Richard Meltzer

THERE ARE NOT ENOUGH OF US

How much verse is magnificent?
Point oh oh oh oh one per cent.
How much poetry is second-rate?
Around point oh oh oh oh eight.
How much verse is botched hotch-potch?
Ninety-eight per cent by my watch.
How much poetry simply bores?
None of mine and all of yours.

Adrian Mitchell

FIRST HAIKU OF SPRING

cuck oo cuck oo cuck
oo cuck oo cuck oo cuck oo
cuck oo cuck oo cuck

Roger McGough

THE TRADITIONAL GRAMMARIAN AS POET

Haiku, you ku, he,
She, or it kus, we ku, you
Ku, they ku. Thang ku.

Ted Hipple

ROBINSON CRUSOE

Wrecked castaway
  On lonely strand
Works hard all day
  To tame the land,
Takes times to pray;
  Makes clothes by hand.

For eighteen years
  His skill he plies,
Then lo! A footprint
  He espies –
'Thank God it's Friday!'
  Crusoe cries.

Take heart from his
  Example, chums:
Work hard, produce;
  Complete your sums;
Eventually,
  Friday comes.

Maurice Sagoff

MELVILLE'S 'TREASURE ISLAND'

Young Hawkins tells me that the ship is bottomless,
but I haven't been below to check.
We sent a man to the crow's nest a week ago,
and he hasn't been back.

This feels like a big ship.

We seem to be stuck
to the harbour walls.
I don't think we're even floating.

Maybe we are becalmed (this
is my first voyage); how
can we find Captain Kidd's gold
if we do not move?

Blind Pugh stands on the bridge
holding an ear-trumpet,
listening for treasure.

This is my first voyage
but I thought that, on a ship,
there was at least the *sensation*
of movement.

I may be wrong.

Tomorrow
he opens the map.

Ian McMillan

A MARKED MAN

December.
A boy named
'Grooly' Pugh
skates over
the wintry
school tarmac.
'Sir, for you,'

and hands me
a paper ball,
a damp clot
then slopes off,
slithering.
Hail and sleet
like grapeshot.

Numb fingered
I unfold
a moist sheet
and there see
(shivering,
my bones cold)
the black spot.

Wes Magee

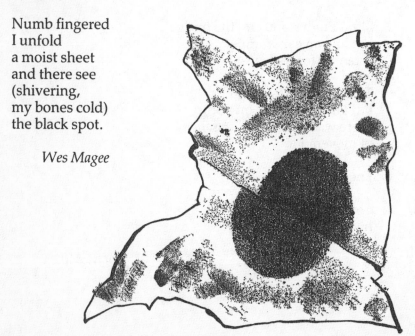

ANCHORED

Our anchor's too big for our ship,
So we're sittin' here tryin' to think.
If we leave it behind we'll be lost.
If we haul it on board, we will sink.
If we sit and keep talkin' about it,
It will soon be too late for our trip.
It sure can be rough on a sailor
When the anchor's too big for the ship.

Shel Silverstein

XMAS FOR THE BOYS

A clockwork skating Wordsworth on the ice,
An automatic sermonising Donne,
A brawling Marlowe shaking out the dice,
A male but metaphysical Thom Gunn.
Get them all now – the latest greatest set
Of all the Poets, dry to sopping wet.

A mad, ferocious, disappointed Swift
Being beaten by a servant in the dark.
Eliot going up to Heaven in a lift,
Shelley going overboard, just for a lark.
Although the tempo and the talent varies
Now is the time to order the whole series.

An electronic Milton, blind as a bat,
A blood-spitting consumptive Keats,
Tennyson calmly raising a tall hat,
Swinburne being whipped in certain dark back streets.
All working models, correct from head to toe –
But Shakespeare's extra, as you ought to know.

Gavin Ewart

I DID A BAD THING ONCE

I did a bad thing once.
I took this money from my mother's purse
For bubble gum.
What made it worse,
She bought me some
For being good, while I'd been vice versa
So to speak – that made it worser.

Allan Ahlberg

A BOY'S BEST FRIEND

The exercise book fell open.
Open at a page on which I'd written poems.
Like some comic French detective, you
picked it up, my mother,
scrutinized one poem, then gently closed
the cover.
'What's behind all this, then?'
you asked with arched eyebrows.
'Are you unhappy, then?
You never said, but then you always were
quiet, even as a baby.'
I made some excuse about bad company,
you know, mixing with some of the grammar
school boys, ideas above my station and all that.

You promised not to tell anyone about our little
secret,
but then one Christmas, when you'd had a little
too much to drink,
you dragged me into the family's gaze and said,
'Here, what do you think?
Our Philip's been writing poems, go on, Phil,
read us one.'
Then,
'No need to get upset, dear, it's just a bit
of fun.'

Paul Camp

THE LESSON

I'll tell you what now little brother
I'm going to teach you something
you'll never ever forget.

You go half way upstairs that's right.
You turn round you shut your eyes.
You keep them shut tight.

Now on the count of five
now I want you to jump.
Now is that clear.

Don't be scared little brother.
I'll be standing at the bottom here
to catch you so be brave.

1 . . . 2 . . . 3 . . . 4 . . .

Five I said I'd teach you something
this is it don't ever trust anybody.
When you're older you'll thank me for it.

Shut up.

Brian McCabe

THE LEADER

I wanna be the leader
I wanna be the leader
Can I be the leader?
Can I? I can?
Promise? Promise?
Yippee, I'm the leader
I'm the leader

OK what shall we do?

Roger McGough

TOO FAST TO LIVE, TOO YOUNG TO WORK

I'm the James Dean of the dole queue
You've got to admire my cheek –
Trying to work out how to live fast and die young
on seventeen-fifty a week.

A legend in my own cubicle
All alone, never one of the mob
I'm the James Dean of the dole queue
A rebel without a job.

Mark Jones

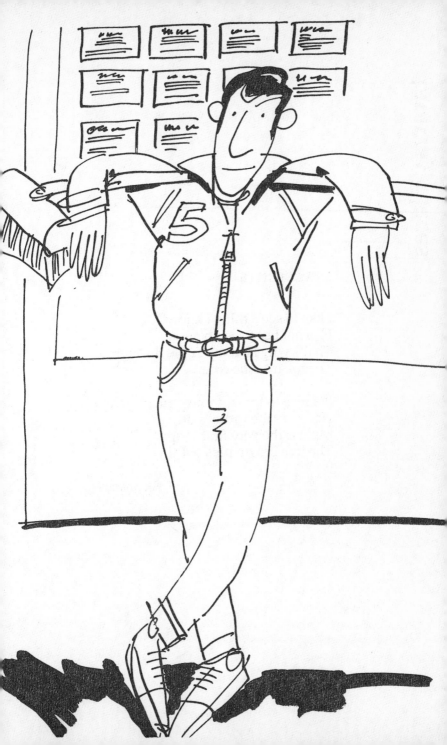

NEW SIGHTS

I like to see a thing I know
Has not been seen before;
That's why I cut my apple through
To look into the core.

It's nice to think, though many an eye
Has seen the ruddy skin,
Mine is the very first to spy
The five brown pips within.

Anonymous

A LUNATIC'S LONDON

Edgware Rumpkin to Euston Squeaker,
I flit about like a bat,
Oxford Circles or Parson's Grievance,
Nobody knows where I'm at –
Nerdsbridge or Nutter's Hill, Uncle or Beercan,
Baconflitch, Byron's Cat!

Moron's Town Crescent, Mopping, Wimbledog,
I'm at the end of the line,
Fluffwell Park, Flappum or Flopping,
All of these places are mine –
You've never heard of them, I've never heard of them,
That's what makes it so fine!

Vicarlily and Cloister Square,
It's an Underground alien land,
Who lives at these places, Dwarfs or Dandelions?
Just let me take your hand,
We'll charge about London on Underground railways –
Then you will understand!

NOTE: *This lunatic, hopelessly confused, seems to be referring to the following London Underground Stations: Edgware Road, Euston Square, Oxford Circus, Parson's Green, Knightsbridge, Notting Hill Gate, Angel, Barbican, Beaconsfield, Baron's Court, Mornington Crescent, Wimbledon, Tufnell Park, Clapham (North or South), Piccadilly, Leicester Square. Exactly what or where Mopping and Flopping are, we shall never know. Wapping, perhaps?*

Gavin Ewart

THE FASTEST TRAIN IN THE WORLD

Tokyo to Kyoto
  tokyotokyoto
kyotokyotokyotokyo
  tokyotokyoto

     Keith Bosley

There was a young girl of Asturias
Whose temper was frantic and furious
She used to throw eggs
At her grandmother's legs –
A habit unpleasant and curious

     Anonymous

There was an old person of Fratton
Who would go to church with his hat on.
'If I wake up,' he said,
'With a hat on my head,
I will know that it hasn't been sat on.'

Anonymous

OF PYGMIES, PALMS AND PIRATES

Of pygmies, palms and pirates,
Of islands and lagoons,
Of blood-bespotted frigates,
Of crags and octoroons,
Of whales and broken bottles,
Of quicksands cold and grey,
Of ullages and dottles,
I have no more to say.

Of barley, corn and furrows,
Of farms and turf that heaves
Above such ghostly burrows
As twitch on summer eves
Of fallow-land and pasture,
Of skies both pink and grey,
I made a statement last year
And have no more to say.

Mervyn Peake

O'ER SEAS THAT HAVE NO BEACHES

O'er seas that have no beaches
To end their waves upon,
I floated with twelve peachès,
A sofa and a swan.

The blunt waves crashed above us
The sharp waves burst around,
There was no one to love us,
No hope of being found –

Where, on the notched horizon
So endlessly a-drip,
I saw all of a sudden
No sign of any ship.

Mervyn Peake

THE TROUBLE WITH GERANIUMS

The trouble with geraniums
is that they're much too red!
The trouble with my toast is that
it's far too full of bread.

The trouble with a diamond
is that it's much too bright.
The same applies to fish and stars
and the electric light.

The trouble with the stars I see
lies in the way they fly.
The trouble with myself is all
self-centred in the eye.

The trouble with my looking-glass
is that it shows me, me:
there's trouble in all sorts of things
where it should never be.

Mervyn Peake

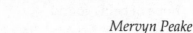

AMERICANS

Americans have very small vocabularies.
They don't understand words like 'constabularies'.
If you went up to a cop in New York and said
'I perceive you are indigenous!' he would hit you on the
                                                    head.

Gavin Ewart

SCOUTS

Pontiac! Little Crow!
Joseph! Red Cloud!
Black Kettle!
Geronimo! Cochise! Crazy Horse!
Tecumseh! Powhatan!
Atahualpa!
Quetzalcoatl!

you're right
– this isn't Walsall, Staffs.

Martin Hall

SPELLING

If an S and an I and an O and a U with an X at the end
spells Sioux,
And an E and a Y and an E spells eye –
Pray what is a speller to do?
If an S and an I and a G and an H and an E and a D
spells sighed,
Pray what is there left for a speller to do but –
To go and commit Sioux-eye-sighed?

Anonymous

BILLY THE KID

Billy was a bad man
And carried a big gun,
He was always chasing women
And kept 'em on the run.

He shot men every morning
Just to make a morning meal –
If his gun ran out of bullets
He killed them with cold steel.

He kept folks in hot water,
And he stole from many a stage,
When his gut was full of liquor
He was always in a rage.

But one day he met a man
Who was a whole lot badder –
And now he's dead –
And we ain't none the sadder.

Anonymous

ARIZONA NATURE MYTH

Up in the heavenly saloon
Sheriff sun and rustler moon
Gamble, stuck in the sheriff's mouth
The fag end of an afternoon.

There in the bad town of the sky
Sheriff, nervy, wonders why
He's let himself wander so far West
On his own; he looks with a smoky eye

At the rustler opposite turning white,
Lays down a king for Law, sits tight
Bluffing. On it that crooked moon
Plays an ace and shoots for the light.

Spurs, badge and uniform red,
(It looks like blood, but he's shamming dead),
Down drops the marshal, and under cover
Crawls out dogwise, ducking his head.

But Law that don't get its man ain't Law.
Next day, faster on the draw,
Sheriff creeping up from the other side
Blazes his way in through the back door.

But moon's not there. He's ridden out on
A galloping phenomenon,
A wonder horse, quick as light.
Moon's left town. Moon's clean gone.

James Michie

FRANK CAREW MACGRAW

The name of Frank Carew Macgraw
Was notorious in the West,
Not as the fastest on the draw
But cause he only wore a vest.

Yes just a vest and nothing more!
Through the Wild and Woolly West,
They knew the name of Frank Macgraw
Cause he only wore a vest.

Oh! His nether parts swung wild and free
As on his horse he sat.
He wore a vest and nothing else –
Oh! except a cowboy hat.

Yes! naked from the waist he rode –
He did not give two hoots!
Frank Macgraw in hat and vest
Oh! and a pair of boots.

But nothing else – no! not a stitch!
As through the cactus he
Rode on his horse, although of course
He did protect his knee

With leather leggings – but that's all!
No wonder that his name
Was infamous throughout the West
And spoken of with shame.

Actually he *did* wear pants
On Sunday, and it's true
He also wore them other days –
And sometimes he wore two!

And often in an overcoat
You'd see him riding by,
But as he went men shook their heads
And ladies winked their eye,

For *everyone* knew Frank Macgraw
Throughout the Old Wild West –
Not because he broke the law
But cause he *only* wore a vest!

Terry Jones

THE PRETTY YOUNG THING

A pretty young thing from St Paul's
Wore a newspaper gown to a ball.
   The dress caught on fire
   And burned her attire
Front page, sporting section and all.

Anonymous

AT THE HOUSEFLY PLANET

Upon the housefly planet
the fate of the human is grim:
for what he does here to the housefly,
the fly does there unto him.

To paper with honey cover
the humans there adhere,
while others are doomed to hover
near death in vapid beer.

However, one practice of humans
the flies will not undertake:
they will not bake us in muffins
nor swallow us by mistake.

Christian Morgenstern

ON SOME OTHER PLANET

On some other planet
near some other star,
there's a music-loving alien
who has a green estate car.

On some other planet
on some far distant world,
there's a bright sunny garden
where a cat lies curled.

On some other planet
a trillion miles away,
there are parks and beaches
where the young aliens play.

On some other planet
in another time zone,
there are intelligent beings
who feel very much alone.

On some other planet
one that we can't see,
there must be one person
who's a duplicate of me.

John Rice

NUTTY NURSERY RHYMES

'Jump over the moon?' the cow declared,
  'With a dish and a spoon. Not me.
I need a suit and a rocket ship
  And filmed by the BBC.

'I want a roomy capsule stall
  For when I blast away,
And an astronaut as a dairymaid
  And a bale of meadow hay.'

She gave a twitch of her lazy rump,
  'Space travel takes up time.
I certainly don't intend to jump
  For a mad old nursery rhyme.'

Max Fatchen

THE OWL AND THE ASTRONAUT

The owl and the astronaut
Sailed through space
In their intergalactic ship
They kept hunger at bay
With three pills a day
And drank through a protein drip.
The owl dreamed of mince
And slices of quince
And remarked how life had gone flat;
'It may be all right
To fly faster than light
But I preferred the boat and the cat.'

Gareth Owen

SHED IN SPACE

My Grandad Lewis
On my mother's side
Had two ambitions.
One was to take first prize
For shallots at the village show
And the second
Was to be a space commander.

Every Tuesday
After I'd got their messages,
He'd lead me with a wink
To his garden shed
And there, amongst the linseed
And the sacks of peat and horse manure
He'd light his pipe
And settle in his deck chair.
His old eyes on the blue and distant
That no one else could see,
He'd ask,
'Are we A O.K. for lift off?'
Gripping the handles of the lawn mower
I'd reply:
'A O.K.'

And then
Facing the workbench,
In front of shelves of paint and creosote
And racks of glistening chisels
He'd talk to Mission Control.
'Five-Four-Three-Two-One-Zero –
We have lift off.
This is Grandad Lewis talking,
Do you read me?
Britain's first space shed
is rising majestically into orbit
From its launch pad
In the allotments
In Lakey Lane.'

And so we'd fly,
Through timeless afternoons
Till tea time came,
Amongst the planets
And mysterious suns,
While the world
Receded like a dream:
Grandad never won
That prize for shallots,
But as the captain
Of an intergalactic shed
There was no one to touch him.

Gareth Owen

o's

A little boy called Robert Rose,
Whenever reading verse or prose
Would often colour in the O's.
He used a pencil for the job
And made each O an odious blob.

Unhappily for Robert Rose,
He caught a strange disease
Where O's appeared between his toes
And then behind his knees.

His elbow, throat and then his nose
Were slowly overgrown with O's,
Then suddenly, oh woe, alack!
Those ovals went completely black.

He died of course, which only shows
You shouldn't mess around with O's!

Doug Macleod

THE HUNTSMAN

Kagwa hunted the lion,
   Through bush and forest went his spear.
One day he found the skull of a man
   And said to it, 'How did you come here?'
The skull opened its mouth and said
   'Talking brought me here.'

Kagwa hurried home;
   Went to the king's chair and spoke:
'In the forest I found a talking skull.'
   The king was silent. Then he said slowly
'Never since I was born of my mother
   Have I seen or heard of a skull which spoke.'

The king called out his guards:
   'Two of you now go with him
And find this talking skull;
   But if his tale is a lie
And the skull speaks no word,
   This Kagwa himself must die.'

They rode into the forest;
   For days and nights they found nothing.
At last they saw the skull; Kagwa
   Said to it 'How did you come here?'
The skull said nothing. Kagwa implored,
   But the skull said nothing.

The guards said 'Kneel down.'
   They killed him with sword and spear.
Then the skull opened its mouth;
   'Huntsman, how did you come here?'
And the dead man answered
   'Talking brought me here.'

Edward Lowbury

KENNETH

who was too fond of bubble-gum and met an untimely end

The chief defect of Kenneth Plumb
Was chewing too much bubble-gum.
He chewed away with all his might,
Morning, evening, noon and night.
Even (oh, it makes you weep)
Blowing bubbles in his sleep.
He simply couldn't get enough!
His face was covered with the stuff.
As for his teeth – oh, what a sight!
It was a wonder he could bite.
His loving mother and his dad
Both remonstrated with the lad.
Ken repaid them for the trouble
By blowing yet another bubble.

Twas no joke. It isn't funny
Spending all your pocket money
On the day's supply of gum –
Sometimes Kenny felt quite glum.
As he grew, so did his need –
There seemed no limit to his greed:
At ten he often put away
Ninety seven packs a day.

Then at last he went too far –
Sitting in his father's car,
Stuffing gum without a pause,
Found that he had jammed his jaws.
He nudged his dad and pointed to
The mouthful that he couldn't chew.
'Well, spit it out if you can't chew it!'
Ken shook his head. He couldn't do it.
Before long he began to groan –
The gum was solid as a stone.
Dad took him to a builder's yard;
They couldn't help. It was too hard.
They called a doctor and he said,
'This silly boy will soon be dead.
His mouth's so full of bubble-gum
No nourishment can reach his tum.'

Remember Ken and please do not
Go buying too much you-know-what.

Wendy Cope

THE CRUEL NAUGHTY BOY

There was a cruel naughty boy,
  Who sat upon the shore,
A-catching little fishes by
The dozen and the score.

And as they squirmed and wriggled there,
  He shouted loud with glee,
'You surely cannot want to live,
  You're little-er than me.'

Just then with a malicious leer,
    And a capacious smile,
Before him from the water deep
    There rose a crocodile.

He eyed the little naughty boy,
    Then heaved a blubbering sigh,
And said, 'You cannot want to live,
    You're little-er than I.'

The fishes squirm and wriggle still,
    Beside that sandy shore,
The cruel little naughty boy,
    Was never heard of more.

William Cole

FLORADORA DOE

Consider the calamity
of Floradora Doe,
who talked to all her plants, because
she thought it helped them grow,
she recited to her ivy,
to her fennel, ferns, and phlox,
she chatted with her cacti
in their little window box.

She murmured to her mosses,
and she yammered to her yew,
she babbled to her basil,
to her borage and bamboo,
she lectured to her laurels,
to her lilac and her lime,
she whispered to her willows,
and she tittered to her thyme.

She gossiped with a poppy,
and she prattled to a rose,
she regaled her rhododendrons
with a constant stream of prose,
then suddenly, one morning,
every plant keeled over, dead.
'Alas!' moaned Floradora.
'Was it something that I said?'

Jack Prelutsky

THE RUBBER PLANT SPEAKS

Mostly they ignore me,
The white plants who walk.
Or bring me water in their leaves.

I wonder how they feed?
With their stubby roots?
And is their green beneath their skins?

Sometimes they talk to me,
But never listen.
They do not recognize my voice.

No one hears. No one hears.
No, not even him,
The little orange plant that swims.

Jan Dean

YOU'D BETTER BELIEVE HIM

He discovered an old rocking-horse in Woolworth's,
He tried to feed it but without much luck.
So he stroked it, had a long conversation about
The trees it came from, the attics it had visited.
Tried to take it out then
But the store detective he
Called the store manager who
Called the police who in court next morning said
'He acted strangely when arrested,
His statement read simply "I believe in rocking-horses".
We have reason to believe him mad.'
'Quite so,' said the prosecution,
'Bring in the rocking-horse as evidence.'
'I'm afraid it's escaped, sir,' said the store manager,
'Left a hoof-print as evidence
On the skull of the store detective.'
'Quite so,' said the prosecution, fearful
of the neighing
Out in the corridor.

Brian Patten

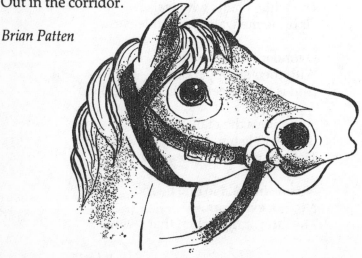

TV

In the house
of Mr and Mrs Spouse
he and she
would watch TV
and never a word
between them spoken
until the day
the set was broken.

Then 'How do you do?'
said he to she,
'I don't believe
that we've met yet.
Spouse is my name.
What's yours?' he asked.

'Why, mine's the same!'
said she to he,
'Do you suppose that we could be – ?'

But the set came suddenly right about,
and so they never did find out.

Eve Merriam

73

THE TIGER

A tiger going for a stroll
Met an old man and ate him whole.

The old man shouted, and he thumped.
The tiger's stomach churned and bumped.

The other tigers said: 'Now really,
We hear your breakfast much too clearly.'

The moral is, he should have chewed.
It does no good to bolt one's food.

Edward Lucie-Smith

A LADY BORN UNDER A CURSE

A lady born under a curse
Used to drive forth each day in a hearse;
    From the back she would wail
    Through a thickness of veil
'Things do not get better but worse.'

Edward Gorey

WHAT'S THE MATTER UP THERE?

'What's the matter up there?'
'Playing soldiers.'
'But soldiers don't make that kind of noise.'
'We're playing the kind of soldier that
makes that kind of noise.'

Carl Sandburg

LO! THE DRUM-MAJOR

Lo! the drum-major in his coat of gold,
His blazing breeches and high-towering cap –
Imperiously pompous, grandly bold,
Grim, resolute, an awe-inspiring chap!
Who'd think this gorgeous creature's only virtue
Is that in battle he will never hurt you?

Ambrose Bierce

UNCLE JAMES

My uncle James
Was a terrible man.
He cooked his wife
In the frying pan.

'She's far too tender
To bake or boil!'
He cooked her up
In peanut oil.

But sometime later –
A month or more –
There came a knock
On my uncle's door.

A great green devil
Was standing there.
He caught my uncle
By the hair.

'Are you the uncle
That cooked his wife,
And leads such a terribly
Wicked life?'

My uncle yowled
Like an old tom cat,
But the devil took him
For all of that.

Oh, take a tip
From my Uncle James!
Don't throw stones
And don't call names.

Just be as good
As ever you can –
And never cook aunts
In a frying pan!

Margaret Mahy

DON'T-CARE

Don't-care didn't care;
   Don't-care was wild.
Don't-care stole plum and pear
   Like any beggar's child.

Don't-care was made to care,
   Don't-care was hung:
Don't-care was put in the pot
   And boiled till he was done.

Anonymous

THE RIGHTEOUS MOTHER

'Wretch!' cried the mother to her infant son.
'You hateful little boy, what have you done?
Killed the white butterfly, of all dear things,
And then pulled off his tiny, fairy wings.
To butterflies this garden is their home –
Here do they dance and kiss the flowers and roam
In happiness and plenty, even as you.
God would be very angry if He knew!'
And while she spoke these salutary words
Her hat displayed two withered humming-birds.

Eden Phillpotts

JACK AND HIS PONY, TOM

Jack had a little pony – Tom;
He frequently would take it from
The stable where it used to stand
And give it sugar with his hand.

He also gave it oats and hay
And carrots twenty times a day
And grass in basketfuls, and greens,
And swedes and mangolds, also beans,
And patent foods from various sources
And bread (which isn't good for horses)
And chocolate and apple-rings
And lots and lots of other things
The most of which do not agree
With Polo Ponies such as he.
And all in such a quantity
As ruined his digestion wholly
And turned him from a Ponopoly
– I mean a Polo Pony – into
A case that clearly must be seen to.

Because he swelled and swelled and swelled.
Which, when the kindly boy beheld,
He gave him medicine by the pail
And malted milk, and nutmeg ale,
And yet it only swelled the more
Until its stomach touched the floor.
And then it heaved and groaned as well
And staggered, till at last it fell
And found it could not rise again.
Jack wept and prayed – but all in vain.
The pony died, and as it died
Kicked him severely in his side.

Moral
Kindness to animals should be
Attuned to their brutality.

Hilaire Belloc

THE PYTHON

A Python I should not advise, –
It needs a doctor for its eyes,
And has the measles yearly.

However, if you feel inclined
To get one (to improve your mind,
And not from fashion merely),

Allow no music near its cage;
And when it flies into a rage
Chastise it, most severely.

I had an aunt in Yucatan
Who bought a Python from a man
And kept it for a pet.

She died, because she never knew
These simple little rules and few; –
The Snake is living yet.

Hilaire Belloc

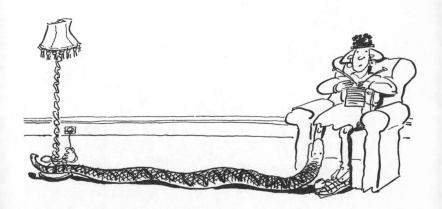

THAT'LL BE ALL RIGHT YOU'LL FIND

James has hated motorists ever since the day
They ran him down and broke his legs in such a heartless
way;
> Oh, My! There are some careless men!
> But what was worse than that was when
> Poor Jimmy heard him say:
> 'That'll be all right you'll find!
> That'll be all right you'll find!
> No more trousers! No more boots!
> Only coat and waistcoat suits
> That'll be all right you'll find!
> You'll walk upon your hands instead
> And have more time to use your head,
> That'll be all right you'll find!'

Mabel fainted right away, they thought that she was dead;
The dentist was shortsighted – pulled her nose clean off her
head!
      Oh My! There are some careless men,
      But what was worse than that was when
      He turned to her and said:
      'That'll be all right you'll find!
      That'll be all right you'll find!
      It was a neat extraction, that,
      And now you'd best put on your hat,
      That'll be all right you'll find!
      No more horrid colds and sniffs!
      No more dirty handkerchiefs!
      That'll be all right you'll find!'

      Rum-Tarrarra! Pom! Pom!

L. de Giberne Sieveking

QUIET FUN

My son Augustus, in the street, one day,
  Was feeling quite exceptionally merry.
A stranger asked him: 'Can you show me, pray,
  The quickest way to Brompton Cemetery?'
'The quickest way? You bet I can!' said Gus,
And pushed the fellow underneath a bus.

Whatever people say about my son,
He does enjoy his little bit of fun.

Harry Graham

TAKE ONE HOME FOR THE KIDDIES

On shallow straw, in shadeless glass,
Huddled by empty bowls, they sleep:
No dark, no dam, no earth, no grass –
Mam, get us one of them to keep.

Living toys are something novel,
But it soon wears off somehow.
Fetch the shoebox, fetch the shovel –
Mam, we're playing funerals now.

Philip Larkin

OUR DOGGY

First he sat, and then he lay,
And then he said: I've come to stay.
And that is how we acquired our doggy Pontz.
He is all right as dogs go, but not quite what one wants.
Because he talks. He talks like you and me.
And he is not you and me, he is made differently.
You think it is nice to have a talking animal?
It is not nice. It is unnatural.

Stevie Smith

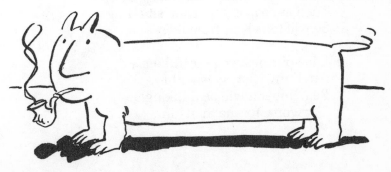

ADVICE TO CHILDREN

Caterpillars living on lettuce
Are the colour of their host:
Look out, when you're eating a salad,
For the greens that move the most.

Close your mouth tight when you're running
As when washing you shut your eyes,
Then as soap is kept from smarting
So will tonsils be from flies.

If in spite of such precautions
Anything nasty gets within,
Remember it will be thinking:
'Far worse for me than him.'

Roy Fuller

HORACE POEM

Much to his Mum and Dad's dismay
Horace ate himself one day.
He didn't stop to say his grace,
He just sat down and ate his face.
'We can't have this!' his Dad declared,
'If that lad's ate, he should be shared.'
But even as he spoke they saw
Horace eating more and more:
First his legs and then his thighs,
His arms, his nose, his hair, his eyes . . .
'Stop him someone!' Mother cried
'Those eyeballs would be better fried!'
But H. was on his second course:
His liver and his lights and lung,
His ears, his neck, his chin, his tongue;
'To think I raised him from the cot
And now he's going to scoff the lot!'
His Mother cried: 'What shall we do?
What's left won't even make a stew . . .'
And as she wept, her son was seen
To eat his head, his heart, his spleen.
And there he lay: a boy no more,
Just a stomach on the floor . . .
None the less, since it *was* his
They ate it – that's what haggis is.

Monty Python

ADVICE TO GROWN UPS AND OTHER ANIMALS......

(Written on a frog by Eric who ate too many worms and died.)

Be very careful
When you're swimming in the sink,
Cos the currents round the plughole,
Are stronger than you think.

Be very, very careful
When you're eating hot barbed wire,
If you gobble, it will prick you,
And you'll suddenly expire.

Be very, very careful
When singing in the rain,
Cos quicker than you think, your clothes will shrink
And you won't get them off again.

Always be very careful
When washing up the pots,
Cos the water makes your fingers soft
And ties them into knots.

And be very, very careful
While swimming through the park,
By the bowls shed and the putting green
There lurks the Dry-Land Shark.

And be very, very careful
While a reading of this book,
For there's something stood behind you
And over your shoulder it looks......

Mike Harding

MY OBNOXIOUS BROTHER

My obnoxious brother Bobby
Has a most revolting hobby;
There, behind the garden wall is
Where he captures creepy-crawlies.

Grannies, aunts and baby cousins
Come to our house in their dozens,
But they disappear discreetly
When they see him smiling sweetly.

For they know, as he approaches,
In his pockets are cockroaches,
Spiders, centipedes and suchlike;
All of which they do not much like.

As they head towards the lobby,
Bidding fond farewells to Bobby,
How they wish he'd change his habits
And keep guinea pigs or rabbits.

But their wishes are quite futile,
For he thinks that bugs are cute. I'll
Finish now, but just remind you:
Bobby could be right behind you!

Colin West

MY LAST NATURE WALK

I strode among the clumihacken
Where scrubble nudges to the barfter
Till I whumped into, hidden in the bracken,
A groolted after-laughter-rafter.

(For milty Wah-Zohs do guffaw
Upon a laughter-rafter perch.
But after laughter they balore
Unto a second beam to gurch.)

Yet here was but one gollamonce!
I glumped upon the after-laughter-rafter.
Where was its other-brother? Oh! My bonce!
The Wah-Zohs blammed it with a laughter-rafter.

Moral: Never gamble on a bramble ramble.

Adrian Mitchell

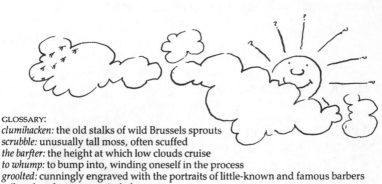

GLOSSARY:
clumihacken: the old stalks of wild Brussels sprouts
scrubble: unusually tall moss, often scuffed
the barfter: the height at which low clouds cruise
to whump: to bump into, winding oneself in the process
groolted: cunningly engraved with the portraits of little-known and famous barbers
milty: clean but mean-minded
Wah-Zohs: French birds, sometimes spelt Oiseaux
to balore: to hover fatly downwards
to gurch: to recover from cheerfulness
gollamonce: a thing that is sought for desperately, although there is no good reason for finding it.
to glump: to glump
to blam: to shonk on the cloddle

93

THE FRIENDLY CINNAMON BUN

Shining in his stickiness and glistening with honey,
Safe among his sisters and his brothers on a tray,
With raisin eyes that looked at me as I put down my money,
There smiled a friendly cinnamon bun, and
    this I heard him say:

'It's a lovely, lovely morning, and the world's a
    lovely place;
I know it's going to be a lovely day.
I know we're going to be good friends; I like
    your honest face;
Together we might go a long, long way.'

The baker's girl rang up the sale, 'I'll wrap your
    bun,' said she.
'Oh no, you needn't bother,' I replied.
I smiled back at that cinnamon bun and ate
    him, one two three,
And walked out with his friendliness inside.

Russell Hoban

I'D LIKE TO BE A TEABAG

I'd like to be a teabag,
And stay at home all day –
And talk to other teabags
In a teabag sort of way . . .

I'd love to be a teabag,
And lie in a little box –
And never have to wash my face
Or change my dirty socks . . .

I'd like to be a teabag,
An Earl Grey one perhaps,
And doze all day and lie around
With Earl Grey kind of chaps.

I wouldn't have to do a thing,
No homework, jobs or chores –
Comfy in my caddy
Of teabags and their snores.

I wouldn't have to do exams,
I needn't tidy rooms,
Or sweep the floor or feed the cat
Or wash up all the spoons.

I wouldn't have to do a thing,
A life of bliss – you see . . .
Except that once in all my life

I'd make a cup of tea!

Peter Dixon

I'D RATHER BE A SAUSAGE

I'd rather be a sausage
Than a British Man of War,
Or a Caterpillar with a broken arm.
Corduroy braces are all very well,
And give no immediate cause for alarm.
But the sausage is a mighty beast,
Who serves only to please.
In fact, he is the mightiest there is.
Content to lie in frying pans
For ages at a stretch
Singing Sizzle Sizzle Sizzle Sizzle Sizz!

Billy Connolly

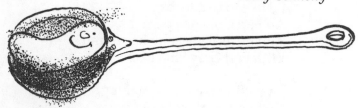

FISH TOES

Think of those yummy fish fingers,
Think of the millions you eat –
Then think of the billions and trillions and zillions
You'd swallow if fishes had FEET!

Roger Woddis

JOHN KEATS EATS HIS PORRIDGE

It was hot enough to blister
The red paint of his mouth.
But if he let it lie there, glistening,
then clipped segments from the circumference,
it slid down like a soggy bobsleigh.

Grey as November, united as the Kingdom
but the longer he stared into that disc of porridge
the more clearly he traced
under the molten sugar
the outline of each flake of oatmeal.

When the milk made its slow blue-tinted leap
    from jug to bowl
the porridge became an island.
John's spoon vibrated in his hand.
The island became a planet.
He made continents, he made seas.

This is strange porridge.
Eat it all up.

Adrian Mitchell

RATTLESNAKE MEAT

A gourmet challenged me to eat
A tiny bit of rattlesnake meat,
Remarking, 'Don't look horror-stricken,
You'll find it tastes a lot like chicken.'
It did.
Now chicken I cannot eat
Because it tastes like rattlesnake meat.

Ogden Nash

RHINOCEROS STEW

If you want to make a rhinoceros stew
all in the world that you have to do
is skin a rhinoceros, cut it in two
and stew it and stew it and stew it.

When it's stewed so long that you've quite forgot
what it is that's bubbling in the pot
dish it up promptly, serve it hot
and chew it and chew it and chew it

and chew it and chew it and chew it
and chew it and chew it and chew it.

AND CHEW IT AND CHEW IT AND CHEW IT

Mildred Luton

VEGETARIANS

Vegetarians are cruel unthinking people.
Everybody knows that a carrot screams when grated
That a peach bleeds when torn apart.
Do you believe an orange insensitive
to thumbs gouging out its flesh?
That tomatoes spill their brains
painlessly? Potatoes, skinned alive
and boiled, the soil's little lobsters.
Don't tell me it doesn't hurt
when peas are ripped from their overcoats,
the hide flayed off sprouts,
cabbage shredded, onions beheaded.

Throw in the trowel and lay down the hoe.
Mow no more. Let my people go!

Roger McGough

99

BANANAS

They have made the colour yellow
famous for its shape.

I like the way their skins unzip
and are vital, in cartoon strips
for unfooting the escapes
of innocent villains.

Their word is a friendly name
for madness.

They have no pips and thus
may be chewed without indignity
or teeth.

They give the sedate fruitbowl
its brazen smile.

Brian McCabe

THE PRUNE

Some base their claims
On tang alone,
But I admire a fruit
That does a job.

Robert Shure

THE HARDEST THING TO DO IN THE WORLD

is stand in the hot sun
at the end of a long queue for ice creams
watching all the people who've just bought theirs
coming away from the queue
giving their ice creams their very first lick.

Michael Rosen

MASHED POTATO/LOVE POEM

If I ever had to choose between you
and a third helping of mashed potato,
(whipped lightly with a fork
not whisked,
and a little pool of butter
melting in the middle . . .)

I think
I'd choose
the mashed potato.

But I'd choose you next.

Sidney Hoddes

IF YOU'RE NO GOOD AT COOKING

If you're no good at cooking,
Can't fry or bake,

Here's something you
Can always make. Take

Three very ordinary
Slices of bread:

Stack the second
On the first one's head.

Stack the third
On top of that.

There! Your three slices
Lying pat.

So what have you got?
A BREAD SANDWICH,

That's what!
Why not?

Kit Wright

GREEDYGUTS

I sat in the café and sipped at a Coke.
There sat down beside me a WHOPPING great bloke
Who sighed as he elbowed me into the wall:
'Your trouble, my boy, is your belly's too small!
Your bottom's too thin! Take a lesson from me:
I may not be nice, but I'm great, you'll agree,
And I've lasted a lifetime by playing this hunch:
The bigger the breakfast, the larger the lunch!

The larger the lunch, then the huger the supper.
The deeper the teapot, the vaster the cupper.
The fatter the sausage, the fuller the tea.
The MORE on the table, the BETTER FOR ME!'

His elbows moved in and his elbows moved out,
His belly grew bigger, chins wobbled about,
As forkful by forkful and plate after plate,
He ate and he ate and he ate and he ATE!

I hardly could breathe, I was squashed out of shape,
So under the table I made my escape.
'Aha!' he rejoiced, 'when it's put to the test,
The fellow who's fattest will come off the best!
Remember, my boy, when it comes to the crunch:
The bigger the breakfast, the larger the lunch!

The larger the lunch, then the huger the supper.
The deeper the teapot, the vaster the cupper.
The fatter the sausage, the fuller the tea.
The MORE on the table, the BETTER FOR ME!'

A lady came by who was scrubbing the floor
With a mop and a bucket. To even the score,
I lifted that bucket of water and said,
As I poured the whole lot of it over his head:

'*I've* found all my life, it's a pretty sure bet:
The FULLER the bucket, the WETTER YOU GET!'

Kit Wright

BABY TOODLES

Alphabet noodles
For Baby Toodles . . .
Alphabet noodles!

HEY!
What's Toodles about?
Why, she's spitting them out!

Mama said,
(As she walloped her over the head)
'Toodles! . . .
Those wonderful alphabet noodles!
I'll send you to bed . . .
That's what I'll do,
At the very next *word* out of you!'

Joseph S. Newman

THERE WAS A YOUNG LADY FROM ICKENHAM

There was a young lady from Ickenham
Who went on a bus-trip to Twickenham.
She drank too much beer,
Which made her feel queer,
So she took off her boots and was sick-in-'em.

Anonymous

LIKE A BEACON

In London
every now and then
I get this craving
for my mother's food
I leave art galleries
in search of plantains
saltfish/sweet potatoes

I need this link

I need this touch
of home
swinging my bag
like a beacon
against the cold

Grace Nichols

UNCLE ED'S HEADS

Fame was a claim of Uncle Ed's,
Simply because he had three heads,
Which, if he'd only had a third of,
I think he would never have been heard of.

Ogden Nash

MARVO

Marvo the Magician
said, 'Young man, come over here
please put this coin inside your hand
and I'll make it disappear.'
He did.
And the one handed young man went home.

David Wood

THIS IS THE HAND

This is the hand
that touched the frost
that froze my tongue
and made it numb

this is the hand
that cracked the nut
that went in my mouth
and never came out

this is the hand
that slid round the bath
to find the soap
that wouldn't float

this is the hand
on the hot water bottle
meant to warm my bed
that got lost instead

this is the hand
that held the bottle
that let go of the soap
that cracked the nut
that touched the frost
this is the hand
that never gets lost.

Michael Rosen

OH TO BE

Oh to be a broken leg
In plaster white as chalk
And travel everywhere by crutch
While others have to walk.

Mike Griffin

FIVE LITTLE BROTHERS

5 little brothers set out together
  To journey the livelong day,
In a curious carriage all made of leather
  They hurried away, away!
One big brother, and 3 quite small,
And one wee fellow, no size at all.

The carriage was dark and none too roomy,
And they could not move about;
The 5 little brothers grew very gloomy,
And the wee one began to pout,
Till the biggest one whispered: 'What
                                do you say?
Let's leave the carriage and run away!'

So out they scampered, the 5 together,
And off and away they sped;
When somebody found the carriage of leather,
Oh my, how she shook her head!
Twas her little boy's shoe, as
                            everyone knows,
And the 5 little brothers were 5
                            little toes.

Anonymous

LOST CONTACT

O the vexation
of dropping
a contact lens!

The contact lens
that would help you find
the contact lens
you are looking for
is
the contact lens
you are looking for!

William Cole

I
NEED
CONTACT
L   E   N   S   E   S

like I need a poke in the eye

John Hegley

M – Meaningful

Y – Yes my glasses are meaningful

G – Grip my head at the sides

L – Love is strong so are my glasses

A – Attached to my head at the sides

S – Stop me walking into opticians

S – See through

E – Ever so clean

S – Seven quid

John Hegley

GRANDAD'S GLASSES

We never used to ask questions
about his glasses.
He needed them to see the telly
and that was that
but then one day
he couldn't see the telly anymore
so he didn't need his glasses.
What were we to do?
It seemed wrong to throw away the glasses
and there was no point in burying them with him
because
a. his eyes were shut
and b. none of us believed in telly after death.
We had a family get together about it
and after the big argument
we came up with two possibilities
a. find someone with glasses like grandad's
and give them the glasses
and b. find someone with glasses like grandad's
and sell them the glasses.

John Hegley

A BLINK

A blink, I think, is the same as a wink,
A blink is a wink that grew,
For a *wink* you wink with only one eye,
And a *blink* you wink with two!

Jacqueline Segal

WINK

I took 40 winks
yesterday afternoon
and another 40 today.
In fact I get through
about 280 winks a week.
Which is about 14,560
winks a year.
(The way I'm going on
I'll end up looking like a wink)

Roger McGough

NURSERY RHYME

What do we use to wash our hair?
We use shampoo to wash our hair.
It's tested scientifically for damage to the eyes
by scientists who, in such matters, are acknowledged
to be wise.
Shampoo. Wash hair. Nice, clean habit.
Go to sleep now, darling.
It doesn't hurt the rabbit.

What makes lather in the bath tub?
Soap makes lather in the bath tub.
Rub-a-dub till bubbles bob along the rubber ducks race!
But don't get any in your mouth because soap has a
nasty taste.
Bath time. Slippy soap! Can't quite grab it!
Let's get dried now, darling.
It doesn't hurt the rabbit.

What makes us better when we're ill?
Medicine helps us when we're ill.
Years of research helped to develop every pill you take,
Like that one we gave you when you had a
tummy ache.
Cut knee. Antiseptic. Gently dab it.
Kiss you better, darling.
It doesn't hurt the rabbit.
It doesn't hurt
It doesn't hurt
It doesn't hurt the rabbit.

Carol Ann Duffy

MARIGOLDS

I bought a bottle of Nettle Shampoo
this morning.
When I got home I wondered whether
I shouldn't shampoo
the marigolds
as well.

Adrian Henri

NORMAN NORTON'S NOSTRILS

Oh, Norman Norton's nostrils
are powerful and strong;
Hold on to your belongings
If he should come along.

And do not ever let him
Inhale with all this might,
Or else your pens and pencils
Will disappear from sight.

Right up his nose they'll vanish
Your future will be black.
Unless he gets the sneezes
You'll *never* get them back.

Colin West

THE SNIFFLE

In spite of her sniffle
Isabel's chiffle.
Some girls with a sniffle
Would be weepy and tiffle;
They would look awful,
Like a rained-on waffle,
But Isabel's chiffle
In spite of her sniffle.
Her nose is more red
With a cold in her head,
But then, to be sure,
Her eyes are bluer.
Some girls with a snuffle,
Their tempers are uffle.
But when Isabel's snivelly
She's snivelly civilly,
And when she's snuffly
She's perfectly luffly.

Ogden Nash

121

THE SNIFFLE

A sniffle crouches on the terrace
in wait for someone he can harass.

And suddenly he jumps with vim
upon a man by name of Schrimm.

Paul Schrimm, responding with 'hatchoo,'
is stuck with him the weekend through.

Christian Morgenstern

JOB SATISFACTION

I am a young bacterium
And I enjoy my work
I snuggle into people's food
I lie in wait – I lurk.
They chomp a bit and chew a bit
And say, 'This can't be beaten'
But then in bed they groan and moan,
'I wish I hadn't eaten.'

John Collis

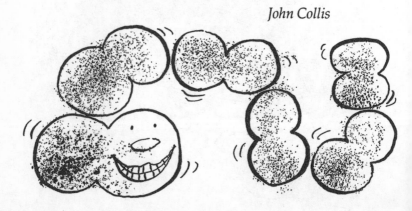

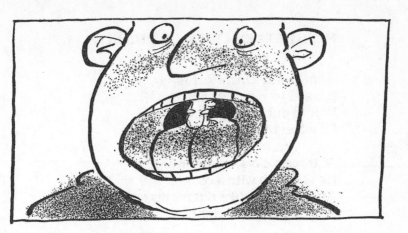

THE BATTLE

Not Alamein or Waterloo:
   The battlefield's my throat!
The enemy, a savage horde
   That swarms across the moat
And storms the citadel –
While the defence is sleeping well.

The white cells then – my bodyguard –
   Join battle with the germs;
Kill millions, but, in turn, are killed;
   The rest are offered terms –
Then, backed by millions more,
Fight on . . . the field, meanwhile, is sore.

At last, with penicillin's aid,
   My throat's at peace again.
Earth, you were sore at Waterloo,
   Hastings and Alamein,
And still have little ease:
Invent your penicillin, please!

Edward Lowbury

NIGHT STARVATION OR THE BITER BIT

At night my Uncle Rufus
(Or so I've heard it said)
Would put his teeth into a glass
Of water by his bed.

At three o'clock one morning
He woke up with a cough,
And as he reached out for his teeth –
They bit his hand right off.

Carey Blyton

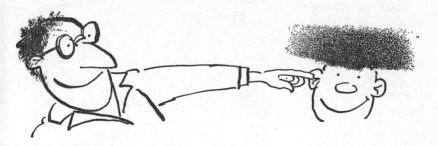

INTELLIGENCE TEST

'What do you use your eyes for?'
The white-coated man enquired.
'I use my eyes for looking,'
Said Toby, '– unless I'm tired.'

'I see. And then you close them,'
Observed the white-coated man.
'Well done. A very good answer.
Let's try another one.

'What is your nose designed for?
What use is the thing to you?'
'I use my nose for smelling,'
Said Toby, 'don't you, too?'

'I do indeed,' said the expert,
'That's what the thing is for.
Now I've another question to ask you,
Then there won't be any more.

'What are your ears intended for?
Those things at each side of your head?
Come on – don't be shy – I'm sure you can say.'
'For washing behind,' Toby said.

Vernon Scannell

EARS

Have you thought to give three cheers
For the usefulness of ears?
Ears will often spring surprises
Coming in such different sizes.
Ears are crinkled, even folded.
Ears turn pink when you are scolded.
Ears can have the oddest habits
Standing rather straight on rabbits.
Ears are little tape-recorders
Catching all the family orders.
Words, according to your mother,
Go in one and out the other.
Each side of your head you'll find them.
Don't forget to wash behind them.
Precious little thanks they'll earn you
Hearing things that don't concern you.

Max Fatchen

PUT THAT RABBIT DOWN AND COME AND EAT YOUR DINNER

126

A HANDSOME YOUNG FELLOW CALLED FREARS

A handsome young fellow called Frears
Was attracted to girls by their ears.
He'd traverse the globe
For a really nice lobe,
And the sight would reduce him to tears.

Michael Palin

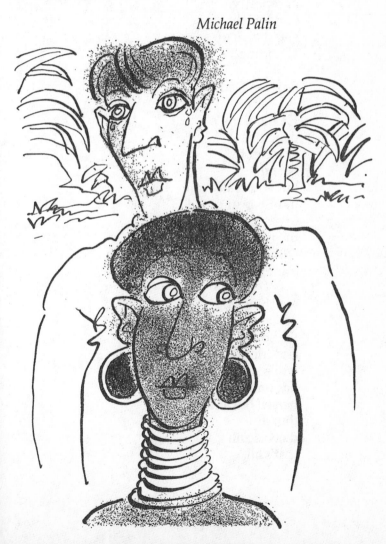

GIVE UP SLIMMING, MUM

My mum
is short
and plump
and pretty
and I wish
she'd give up
slimming.

So does Dad.

Her cooking's
delicious –
you can't
beat it –
but you really can
hardly bear
to eat it –
the way she sits
with her eyes
brimming,

watching you
polish off
the spuds
and trimmings
while she
has nothing
herself but a small
thin dry
diet biscuit:
that's all.

My Mum
is short
and plump
and pretty
and I wish
she'd give up
slimming.

So does Dad.

She says she
looks as though
someone had
sat on her –
BUT WE LIKE MUM
WITH A BIT
OF FAT ON HER!

Kit Wright

. . . AND A FAT POEM

Fat is
as fat is
as fat is

Fat does
as fat thinks

Fat feels
as fat please

Fat believes

      Fat is to butter
      as milk is to cream
      fat is to sugar
      as pud is to steam

Fat is a dream
in times of lean

      fat is a darling
      a dumpling
      a squeeze
      fat is cuddles
      up a baby's sleeve

      and fat speaks for itself

Grace Nichols

HUSBANDS AND WIVES

Husbands and wives
　　With children between them
Sit in the subway;
　　So I have seen them.

One word only
　　From station to station;
So much talk for
　　So close a relation.

Miriam Hershenson

UNCLE FUDGE TOLD LIES

My Uncle Fudge told lies!
Was a deep sea diver once he said,
Kicked fishes and chips on the ocean bed
Played gin rummy and snap with an octoped
For a stake of chocolate mice.

My Uncle Fudge told fibs!
Said he sailed the main with Captain Hook
When the food got bad they keel-hauled the cook,
They said 'The burned jelly fish we could overlook
But you singed Sid Kidd's squid you did.'

My Uncle Fudge told whoppers!
Said he was swallowed by a whale on Blackpool shore
And lived in its innards for twelve month or more
And on long afternoons to stop himself getting bored
He scrubbed the old Leviathan's choppers!

My Uncle Fudge tergiversated!
Said he could eat worms without going mad,
Said he'd done so since he was a lad,
Said with butterfly sauce they didn't taste bad
And he'd eat them until he was sated! . . .

My Uncle Fudge told untruths!
Said that when that he had been a youth
He'd fought with an uncouth wiffenpoof
That had gnawed a big hole in his grandad's roof
So he'd knocked out one of its tooths!

My Uncle Fudge told stretchers!
Said he'd once been marooned in the Sahara
With only a jar of cascara
And an onyx and ormolu candelabra
Did we disbelieve him . . . you betchas.

My Uncle Fudge he lied!
Said he would live till the end of time,
Till three hundred thousand zillion and seventy nine!
And how did I know in the end he was lying
Last Wednesday at tea
He choked on a pea
And said 'O.K. I own up'
And died.

Mike Harding

CHRISTMAS THANK YOU'S

Dear Auntie
Oh, what a nice jumper
I've always adored powder blue
and fancy you thinking of
orange and pink
for the stripes
how clever of you

Dear Uncle
The soap is
terrific
So
useful
and such a kind thought and
how did you guess that
I'd just used the last of
the soap that last Christmas brought

Dear Gran
Many thanks for the hankies
Now I really can't wait for the flu
and the daisies embroidered
in red round the 'M'
for Michael
how
thoughtful of you

Dear Cousin
What socks!
and the same sort you wear
so you must be
the last word in style
and I'm certain you're right that the
luminous green
will make me stand out a mile

Dear Sister
I quite understand your concern
it's a risk sending jam in the post
But I think I've pulled out
all the big bits
of glass
so it won't taste too sharp
spread on toast

Dear Grandad
Don't fret
I'm delighted
So *don't* think your gift will
offend
I'm not at all hurt
that you gave up this year
and just sent me
a fiver
to spend

Mick Gowar

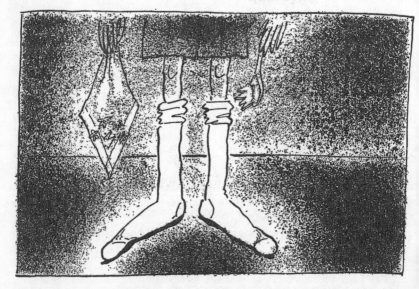

SISTERS

If only I hadn't had sisters
How much more romantic I'd be
But my sisters were such little blisters
That all women are sisters to me.

Anonymous

MY SISTER LAURA

My sister Laura's bigger than me
And lifts me up quite easily.
I can't lift her, I've tried and tried;
She must have something heavy inside.

Spike Milligan

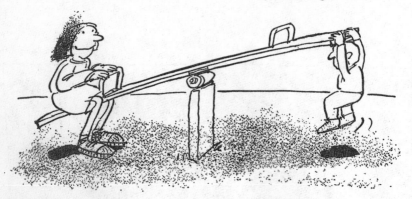

SAMMY

I wish I was our Sammy
Our Sammy's nearly ten.
He's got two worms and a catapult
An' he's built a underground den.
But I'm not allowed to go in there,
I have to stay near the gate,
'Cos me Mam says I'm only seven,
But I'm not, I'm nearly eight!

I sometimes hate our Sammy,
He robbed me toy car y' know,
Now the wheels are missin' an' the top's broke off,
An' the bleedin' thing won' go.

An' he said when he took it, it was just like that,
But it wasn't, it went dead straight,
But y' can't say nott'n when they think y' seven
An' y' not, y' nearly eight.

I wish I was our Sammy,
Y' wanna see him spit,
Straight in y' eye from twenty yards
An' every time a hit.
He's allowed to play with matches,
And he goes to bed dead late,
And I have to go at seven,
Even though I'm nearly eight.

Y' know our Sammy,
He draws nudey women,
Without arms, or legs, or even heads
In the baths, when he goes swimmin'.
But I'm not allowed to go to the baths,
Me Mam says I have to wait,
'Cos I might get drowned, cos I'm only seven,
But I'm not, I'm nearly eight.

Y' know our Sammy,
Y' know what he sometimes does?
He wees straight through the letter box
Of the house next door to us.
I tried to do it one night,
But I had to stand on a crate,
'Cos I couldn't reach the letter box
But I will by the time I'm eight.

Willie Russell

EXACTLY LIKE A 'V'

When my brother Tommy
Sleeps in bed with me
He doubles up
And makes
himself
exactly
like
a
V

And 'cause the bed is not so wide
A part of him is on my side.

Abram Bunn Ross

THE PARENT

Children aren't happy with nothing to ignore,
And that's what parents were created for.

Ogden Nash

I WONDER WHY DAD IS SO THOROUGHLY MAD

I wonder why Dad is so thoroughly mad,
I can't understand it at all,
unless it's the bee still afloat in his tea,
or his underwear, pinned to the wall.

Perhaps it's the dye on his favorite tie,
or the mousetrap that snapped in his shoe,
or the pipeful of gum that he found with his thumb,
or the toilet, sealed tightly with glue.

It can't be the bread crumbled up in his bed,
or the slugs someone left in the hall,
I wonder why Dad is so thoroughly mad,
I can't understand it at all.

Jack Prelutsky

MY DAD, YOUR DAD

My dad's fatter than your dad,
Yes, my dad's fatter than yours:
If he eats any more he won't fit in the house,
He'll have to live out of doors.

Yes, but my dad's balder than your dad,
My dad's balder, O.K.,
He's only got two hairs left on his head
And both are turning grey.

Ah, but my dad's thicker than your dad,
My dad's thicker, all right.
He has to look at his watch to see
If it's noon or the middle of the night.

Yes, but my dad's more boring than your dad.
If he ever starts counting sheep
When he can't get to sleep at night, he finds
It's the sheep that go to sleep.

But my dad doesn't mind your dad.
Mine quite likes yours too.
I suppose they don't always think much of us!
That's true, I suppose, that's true.

Kit Wright

141

LAURIE AND DORRIE

The first thing that you'll notice if
    You meet my Uncle Laurie
Is how, whatever else he does,
    He can't stop saying sorry.

He springs from bed at 5 a.m.
    As birds begin to waken,
Cries, 'No offence intended lads –
    Likewise, I hope, none taken!'

This drives his wife, my Auntie Dorrie,
    Mad. It's not surprising
She grabs him by the throat and screeches,
    'Stop apologizing!'

My Uncle, who's a little deaf,
   Says, 'Sorry? Sorry, Dorrie?'
'For goodness' sake,' Aunt Dorrie screams,
   'Stop saying sorry, Laurie!'

'Sorry, dear? Stop saying what?'
   'SORRY!' Laurie's shaken.
'No need to be, my dear,' he says,
   For *no offence is taken*.

Likewise I'm sure that there was none
   Intended on your part.'
'Dear Lord,' Aunt Dorrie breathes, 'what can
   I do, where do I start?'

Then, 'Oh, I *see*,' says Uncle L.,
   'You mean "stop saying sorry"!
I'm sorry to have caused offence –
   Oops! Er . . . *sorry*, Dorrie!'

Kit Wright

CAR ATTACK

On last year's Halloween
A car hit Auntie Jean.
Unhinged by this attack,
My Auntie hit it back.

She hit it with her handbag
And knocked it with her knee.
She socked it with a sandbag
And thumped it with a tree.

On last year's Halloween
A car hit Auntie Jean.
And now, my Auntie's better
But the car is with the wrecker.

Doug Macleod

COUSIN NELL

Cousin Nell
married a frogman
in the hope
that one day
he would turn into
a handsome prince.

Instead he turned into
a sewage pipe
near Gravesend
and was never seen again.

Roger McGough

AUNT ERMINTRUDE

Aunt Ermintrude
was determined to
swim across the Channel.
Each week she'd
practise in the bath
encostumed in flannel.

The tap end
was Cap Gris Nez
the slippy slopes
were Dover. She'd
doggypaddle up and down
vaselined all over.

After 18 months, Aunt Erm was in peak condition.
So, one cold grey morning in March
she boarded the Channel steamer at Dover
went straight to her cabin
climbed into the bath
and urged on by a few well-wishers,
Aunt Ermintrude, completely nude
swam all the way to France.
Vive la tante!

Roger McGough

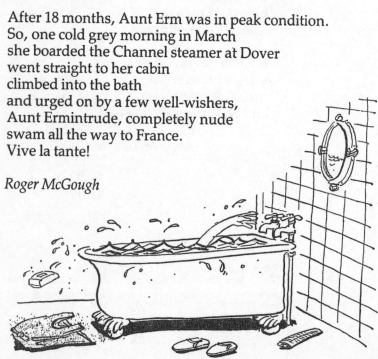

MY AUNT

I take my Aunt out in her pram
I am her grown-up Nephew 'Sam'!
My Grandma's sister married late
And by a stroke of Life's strange fate
Her children all arrived when we
Were roundabout aged Twenty-three.
It is most pleasing for a chap
To bounce his Aunt upon his lap!

Peggy Wood

CHILDREN WITH ADULTS

My auntie gives me a colouring book and crayons.
I choose the picture of the puppies in a wicker basket.
I begin to colour.
After a while Auntie leans over to see what I have done
and says 'you've gone over the lines,
that's what you've done!
What do you think they're there for, eh?
Some kind of statement is it?
Going to be a rebel are we?
Your auntie's given you a nice present
and you've gone and spoilt it.'
I begin to cry.
My uncle gives me a hanky and some blank paper.
'Do some doggies of your own,' he says.
I begin to colour.
When I have done
he looks over
and says they are all very good.
He is lying;
only some of them are.

John Hegley

GRANDMA

My grandmother's a peaceful person, and she loves to sit.
But there never was a grandma who was such a one to knit.

Scarves, caps, suits, socks –
Her needles tick like fifty clocks
But not for you and not for me.
What makes her knit so busily?

All summer wasps toil tirelessly to earn their daily dinner,
Their black and yellow jerseys getting shabbier and thinner.

Grandma knows just how a wasp grows
Weary of its one suit of clothes.
She knits flowered skirts and speckled pants –
Now they can go to the beach or a dance.

Under the ice the goldfish hear December blizzards beating.
They have no fire at all down there, no rooms with central
heating.

So when frost nips the lily roots
Grandma's knitting woolly suits –
Greens, blues, the goldfish adore them!
Winter-long they're thankful for them.

When snowy winds are slicing in through all the little
crannies
The shrubs and birds in our neighbours' gardens envy those
in my granny's.

Her shrubs have scarves and pullovers,
Her birds have ear-muffs over their ears,
And cats that come asking for 'Titbits please'
Go trotting away with little bootees.

A frosty Octopus received a stout eight-fingered mitten.
A Camel whose important hump tended to get frost-bitten

    Has a tea-cosy with tassels on it.
    A grass-snake has a sock with a bonnet.
    Folks can buy clothes at some shop or other.
    The creatures depend on my grandmother.

Ted Hughes

MEN TALK

Women
Rabbit rabbit rabbit women
Tattle and titter
Women prattle
Women waffle and witter

Men Talk. Men Talk.

Women into Girl Talk
About Women's Trouble
Trivia 'n' Small Talk
They yap and they babble

Men Talk. Men Talk.

Women yatter
Women chatter
Women chew the fat, women spill the beans
Women aint been takin'
The oh-so Good Advice in them
Women's Magazines.

A Man Likes A Good Listener.

Oh yeah
I like A Woman
Who likes me enough
Not to nitpick
Not to nag and
Not to interrupt 'cause I call that treason
A woman with the Good Grace
To be struck dumb
By me Sweet Reason. Yes –

A Man Likes a Good Listener

A Real
Man
Likes a Real Good Listener

women yap yap yap
Verbal Diarrhoea is a Female Disease
Woman she spread she rumours round she
Like Philadelphia Cream Cheese.

Oh
Bossy Women Gossip
Girlish Women Giggle
Women natter, women nag
Women niggle niggle niggle

Men Talk.

Men
Think First. Speak Later
Men Talk.

                                        Liz Lochhead

JONAH AND THE WHALE

Well, to start with
It was dark
So dark
You couldn't see
Your hand in front of your face;
And huge
Huge as an acre of farmland.
How do I know?
Well, I paced it out
Length and breadth
That's how.
And if you was to shout
You'd hear your own voice resound,
Bouncing along the ridges of its stomach,
Like when you call out
Under a bridge
Or in an empty hall.
Hear anything?
No not much,
Only the normal
Kind of sounds
You'd expect to hear
Inside a whale's stomach;
The sea swishing far away,
Food gurgling, the wind
And suchlike sounds;
Then there was me screaming for help,
But who'd be likely to hear,
Us being miles from
Any shipping lines
And anyway

Supposing someone did hear,
Who'd think of looking inside a whale?
That's not the sort of thing
That people do.
Smell?
I'll say there was a smell.
And cold. The wind blew in
Something terrible from the South
Each time he opened his mouth
Or took a swallow of some tit bit.
The only way I found
To keep alive at all
Was to wrap my arms
Tight round myself
And race from wall to wall.
Damp? You can say that again;
When the ocean came sluicing in
I had to climb his ribs
To save myself from drowning.
Fibs? You think I'm telling you fibs,
I haven't told the half of it.
Brother
I'm only giving a modest account
Of what these two eyes have seen
And that's the truth on it.
Here, one thing I'll say
Before I'm done –
Catch me eating fish
From now on.

Gareth Owen

A SAIL ON THE SEA

A sail on the sea
Is a thing that suits me,
And I've done some sailing, it's true;
I've been at m' wits end
When sailing to Land's End
And one night – when I'd 'ad one or two –
The Captain came out on the bridge and said, 'Lads!
'We're all doomed . . .
'The 'ole tub's goin' down.
'To the boats. Every man. Except you.' I said,
    'Me?' He said,
'Yes, there's no room, you must drown.'
I said 'Drown?' He said, '*Drown*; the 'ole ship's
    goin' down,
'Don't stand arguin' there,
'I've just told you straight
'There's not room for you mate,
'On the boats or in fact anywhere.
'I know it's upsetting
'But what's the use of fretting?
'We might have lost all of the crew;
'But *now*, as I say,
'We can all get away,
'And only lose one, and that's you.'

Robb Wilton

155

WELL, HARDLY EVER

Never throw a brick at a drownin' man
Outside a grocery store –
Always throw him a bar a soap –
And he'll wash himself ashore.

Anonymous

I SAW YOU

I saw you
looking from your window,
looking at the street below.
I shouted out 'Hallo,
can you come and play?'
on the day
that
I saw you.

I saw you
opening your window,
opening your mouth to speak,
your voice made me feel weak,
malleable as clay
on the day
that
I saw you.

I saw you
leaning from your window
leaning for a better view,
I said, 'What shall we do?'
You said, 'Run away'
on the day
that
I saw you.

Your face shone with excitement
as you looked down at me.
We'd soon be on our own to play,
contented as could be.

I saw you
falling from your window,
falling to the street below
it's quite a way to go,
on the ground you lay
on the day
that
I saw you.

I saw them
rushing to your window,
rushing to the gruesome scene.
You know what this'll mean?
You can't come and play,
nor can I,
you
fell on me.

David Wood

FRAMED IN A FIRST-STOREY WINDER . . .

Framed in a first-storey winder of a burnin' buildin'
Appeared: A Yuman Ead!
Jump into this net, wot we are 'oldin'
And yule be quite orl right!

But 'ee wouldn't jump . . .

And the flames grew Igher and Igher and Igher.
(Phew!)

Framed in a second-storey winder of a burnin' buildin'
Appeared: A Yuman Ead!
Jump into this net, wot we are 'oldin'
And yule be quite orl right!

But 'ee wouldn't jump . . .

And the flames grew Igher and Igher and Igher
(Strewth!)

Framed in a third-storey winder of a burnin' buildin'
Appeared: A Yuman Ead!
Jump into this net, wot we are 'oldin'
And yule be quite orl right!
Honest!

And 'ee jumped . . .

And 'ee broke 'is bloomin' neck!

Anonymous

I'VE GOT MY HEAD STUCK IN THE RAILINGS

I've got my head stuck in the railings,
I've been here since quarter to eight
Some bloke said he'd send for the fire brigade,
If he did then they're seven hours late.

I'm stuck in the stocks like a sideshow
With ev'ryone peering at me,
You'd think I was Chi Chi the panda when
They all throw me stale buns for my tea.

The word spread around pretty quickly
And looters were quick on the scene,
My glasses, my beard and moustache had gone
By the time that the police intervened.

I've had BBC news here to film me
And the ITN popped along too.
And it made me very proud
When before a big crowd
Terry Wogan gave me an interview.

All the bookies are making a small fortune
Off'ring odds on how long I'll be here,
As they shout, 'What am I bet
On how much blood they'll have to let?
Six to one he's going to lose an ear.'

My next of kin came at the double,
My aunts, uncles, granmas and pas.
My mum nudged my dad with a laugh and said
I just knew he'd end up behind bars.
Ha ha ha.

My grandad was much more concerned though
He knew I was going through hell.
He started to tug at the railings but
I'm still here and now he's stuck as well.

I'm praying that someone will help us
Though I don't know who, how or when
But one thing I'm certain I'll never do
Try to steal the crown jewels again.

David Wood

THE UPS AND DOWNS OF THE ELEVATOR CAR

The elevator car in the elevator shaft,
Complained of the buzzer, complained of the draught.
It said it felt carsick as it rose and fell,
It said it had a headache from the ringing of the bell.

'There is spring in the air,' sighed the elevator car.
Said the elevator man, 'You are well-off where you are.'
The car paid no attention but it frowned an ugly frown
                        when
                  up   it
            going   should
                                    be
      started   going
      it   down.
And

Down flashed the signal, but up went the car.
The elevator man cried, 'You are going much too far!'
Said the elevator car, 'I'm doing no such thing.
I'm through with buzzers buzzing, I'm looking for the spring!'

Then the elevator man began to shout and call
And all the people came running through the hall.

The elevator man began to call and shout
'The car won't stop! Let me out! Let me out!'

On went the car past the penthouse door.
On went the car up one flight more.
On went the elevator till it came to the top.
On went the elevator, and it would not stop!

Right through the roof went the man and the car.
And nobody knows where the two of them are!
(Nobody knows but everyone cares,
Wearily, drearily climbing the stairs!)

Now on a summer evening when you see a shooting star
Fly through the air, perhaps it is – that elevator car!

Caroline D. Emerson

EMBRIONIC MEGASTARS

We can play reggae music, funk and skiffle too.
We prefer heavy metal but the classics sometimes do.
We're keen on Tamla-Motown, folk and soul,
But most of all, what we like
Is basic rock and roll.
We can play the monochord, the heptachord and flute,
We're OK on the saxophone and think the glockenspiel is
cute,
We really love the tuba, the balalaika and guitar
And our duets on the clavichord are bound to take us far.
We think castanets are smashing, harmonicas are fun,
And with the ocarina have only just begun.
We've mastered synthesizers, bassoons and violins
As well as hurdy-gurdies, pan-pipes and mandolins.
The tom-tom and the tabor, the trumpet and the drum
We learnt to play in between the tintinnabulum.
We want to form a pop group
And will when we're eleven,
But at the moment Tracey's eight
And I am only seven.

Brian Patten

THE CHARGE OF THE MOUSE BRIGADE

Half an inch, half an inch,
Half an inch onward,
Into Cat Valley
Rode the Six Hundred.

'Forward the Mouse Brigade!
Ravage their fleas!' he said.
'Capture the cheese!' he said.
Onward they thundered.

Claws to the right of them.
Claws to the left of them.
Claws to the front of them.
Pounces unnumbered.

Crash! – through the Catty flanks!
Shattered their fishy ranks!
Captured the Cheddar! thanks
To the Mouse Brigade!
Noble Six Hundred.

Bernard Stone

JUNGLE TIPS

(1) KILLER BEE

If you are bitten by a killer bee, bite it right back. A series of alkaline anti-bodies will be released which you may spit on to the wound, neutralising it. There is also the keen satisfaction of biting its furry little body in two.

(2) PIRANHAS

If you are wading across the Amazon, and a school of piranhas starts to take an interest, hum like mad whilst spilling a bottle of tomato ketchup across the river. They will imagine that you are another bleeding humming-bird, and will shun you as they cannot abide feathers stuck to their teeth.

Ivor Cutler

VYMURA: THE SHADE CARD POEM

Now artistic I aint, but I went to choose paint
'cos the state of the place made me sick.
I got a shade card, consumers-aid card, but it stayed hard to
    pick.
So I asked her advice as to what would look nice,
would blend in and not get on my wick.

She said 'our Vymura is super in Durer,
or see what you think of this new shade, Vlaminck.
But I see that you're choosy . . .
Picasso is newsy . . . that's greyish-greeny-bluesy . . .
Derain's all the rage . . .
that's hot-pink and Fauve-ish . . .
There's Monet . . . that's mauve-ish . . .
And Schwitters,
that's sort-of-a-*beige*.'

She said 'Fellow next door just sanded his floor
and rollered on Rouault and Rothko
His hall, och it's Pollock an' he
did his lounge in soft Hockney
with his cornice picked out in Kokoshka.'

'Now avoid the Van Gogh, you'll not get it off,
the Bonnard is bonny,
you'd be safe with matt Manet,
the Goya is *gorgeous*
or Chagall in eggshell,
but full-gloss Lautrec's sort of tacky.
So stick if you can to satin-finish Cezanne
or Constable . . . that's kind of khaki.
Or the Gainsborough green . . .
and I'd call it hooey to say Cimabue
would never tone in with Soutine.'

'If it looks a bit narrow when you splash on Pissarro
one-coat Magritte covers over.'
She said 'this Hitchens is a nice shade for kitchens
with some Ernst to connect 'em at other end of the spectrum,
Botticelli's lovely in the louvre.
She said 'If it was mine I'd do it Jim Dine . . .
don't think me elitist or snobby . . .
but Filipo Lippi'd
look awfy insipid,
especially in a large-ish lobby!'

Well, I did one wall Watteau, with the skirting Giotto,
and the door and the pelmet in Poussin.
The ceiling's de Kooning,
other walls all in Hals
and the whole place looks quite . . . cavalier,
with the woodwork in Corot –
but I think tomorrow
I'll flat-white it back to Vermeer.

Liz Lochhead

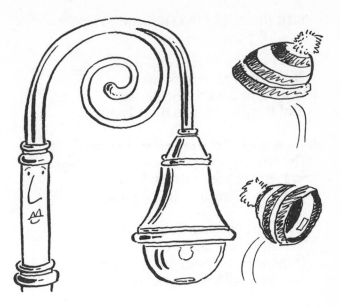

DEAR MAUREEN

Dear Maureen,
I am a lamp-post.
Every Saturday evening at five o'clock
three boys
wearing blue and white scarves
blue and white hats
waving their arms in the air
and shouting,
come my way.
Sometimes they kick me.
Sometimes they kiss me.
What should I do
to get them to make up their minds?
Yours bewilderedly,
Annie Onlight.

Michael Rosen

THE REVOLT OF THE LAMP POSTS

Last night I saw the lamp posts
That light up our back street
Wiggle, and then wriggle
And then, suddenly, they'd feet.

Then they all cleared off and left us,
The whole street in the dark,
So I left the house and followed,
There were millions in the park.

All the lamps from miles around
Had run away tonight,
They were dancing, they were singing,
And they held each other tight.

The king, a big green lamp post
Said 'No more workin' brothers!
We'll leave them humings in the dark
And they'll bump into each other.

Just think about them walkin' round
With black eyes and broke noses
No more dogs to wet your feet
No more rusty toeses!

See, I've been a lamp post all me life, but
Now me mantles growin' dim,
They'll chuck me on the scrap heap
It's a shame! a crime! a sin! . . .

The other lamp posts muttered
And began to hiss and boo,
'Let's march upon the Town Hall
That's what we ought to do!'

The Lord Mayor he was woken
By a terribobble sight,
When he opened up his window
Didn't he get a fright!

There were twenty million lamp posts
And the light as bright as day
And the young lamp posts were shoutin' out
'Free Speech and Equal Pay! –

New Mantles Every Quarter!'
'I agree' the Lord Mayor cried
'To everything you ask for!'
Then he quickly ran inside.

So I watched the lamp posts go back home,
As quickly as they came
And with the first light of the day,
They were in their holes again.

Now there's an old age home for lamp posts
And an old age pension scheme
And every month they're painted
With a coat of glossy green,

New mantles every couple of months,
And they stand up straighter too,
And only the Lord Mayor knows why,
Him, and me, and twenty million lamp posts,

And a couple hundred dogs – and you.

Mike Harding

TREADIN' STEADY

Thrifty an' careful
John William Kaye
Browt up his youngsters
In t' similar way:
When he took 'em out walkin',
He'd cry, 'All together!
Lengthen your strides, lads,
An' save your boot-leather!'

William Beaumont

MI TWO AUNTS

Aunt Emma let us run around,
Aunt Lizzie made us sit;
Aunt Emma used to laugh a lot,
Aunt Lizzie, not a bit.

Aunt Lizzie had a lot to say,
But she talked ovver-mich
O' recent deaths an' buryins'
O' illnesses an' sich.

Aunt Emma made her currant-buns
So sweet an' fat an' nice,
Wi' currants plump an' plentiful
In ivvery tasty slice.

Aunt Lizzie's currant-buns were sad,
They nivver seemed to suit;
We fun' 'em short o' sweetenin',
An' allus short o' fruit.

Aunt Emma spread her butter thick,
Aunt Lizzie spread it thin;
– 'T were mostly to Aunt Emma's house
That we went visitin'!

William Beaumont

JUST ANOTHER AUTUMN DAY

In Parliament, the Minister for Mists
and Mellow Fruitfulness announces,
that owing to inflation and rising costs
there will be no Autumn next year.
September, October and November
are to be cancelled,
and the Government to bring in
the nine-month year instead.
Thus will we all live longer.

Emergency measures are to be introduced
to combat outbreaks of well-being
and feelings of elation inspired by the season.
Breathtaking sunsets will be restricted
to alternate Fridays, and gentle dusks
prohibited. Fallen leaves will be outlawed,
and persons found in possession of conkers,
imprisoned without trial.
Thus will we all work harder.

The announcement caused little reaction.
People either way don't really care
No time have they to stand and stare
Looking for work or slaving away
Just another Autumn day.

Roger McGough

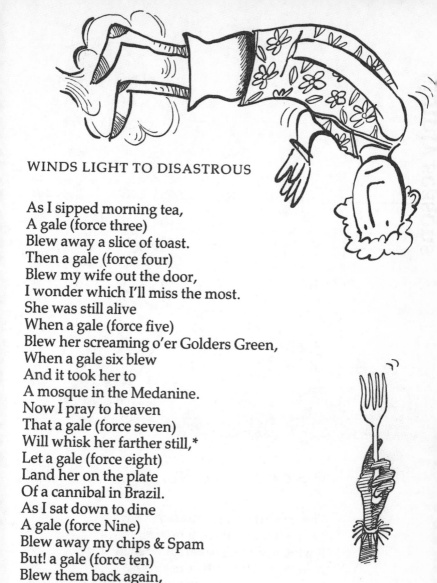

WINDS LIGHT TO DISASTROUS

As I sipped morning tea,
A gale (force three)
Blew away a slice of toast.
Then a gale (force four)
Blew my wife out the door,
I wonder which I'll miss the most.
She was still alive
When a gale (force five)
Blew her screaming o'er Golders Green,
When a gale six blew
And it took her to
A mosque in the Medanine.
Now I pray to heaven
That a gale (force seven)
Will whisk her farther still,*
Let a gale (force eight)
Land her on the plate
Of a cannibal in Brazil.
As I sat down to dine
A gale (force Nine)
Blew away my chips & Spam
But! a gale (force ten)
Blew them back again,
What a lucky man I am!

Spike Milligan

* Father Still, a stationery priest

WINDY

The gale upon our holidays
Was not your passing breeze.
It gave our tents a fearful wrench
And bent the frantic trees.
So, if you've seen a flying tent,
And then observe another,
Please call us at your earliest,
We're also missing mother.

Max Fatchen

BALLOON

```
        a s
       big  as
     ball as round
    as sun . . . I tug
  and pull you when
  you run and when
     wind blows I
       say polite
            ly
             H
              O
           L
            D
              M
                E
                 T
                I
                  G
                   H
                    T
                     L
                      Y.
```

Colleen Thibaudeau

ANCIENT MUSIC

Winter is icummen in,
Lhude sing Goddamm,
Raineth drop and staineth slop,
And how the wind doth ramm!
　　　　　Sing: Goddamm.
Skiddeth bus and sloppeth us,
An ague hath my ham.
Freezeth river, turneth liver,
　　　　Damn you, sing: Goddamm.
Goddamn, Goddamn, 'tis why I am, Goddamm,
　　　　So 'gainst the winter's balm,
Sing goddamm, damm, sing Goddam,
Sing goddamm, sing goddamm, DAMM.

Ezra Pound

NOT A VERY CHEERFUL SONG, I'M AFRAID

There was a gloomy lady,
With a gloomy duck and a gloomy drake,
And they all three wandered gloomily,
Beside a gloomy lake,
On a gloomy, gloomy, gloomy, gloomy, gloomy, gloomy
day.

Now underneath that gloomy lake
The gloomy lady's gone.
But the gloomy duck and the gloomy drake
Swim on and on and on.
On a gloomy, gloomy, gloomy, gloomy, gloomy, gloomy
day.

Adrian Mitchell

IT'S NEVER FAIR WEATHER

I do not like the winter wind
That whistles from the North.
My upper teeth and those beneath
They jitter back and forth.
Oh, some are hanged, and some are skinned,
And others face the winter wind.

I do not like the summer sun
That scorches the horizon.
Though some delight in Fahrenheit,
To me it's deadly pizen.
I think that life would be more fun
Without the simmering summer sun.

I do not like the signs of spring,
The fever and the chills,
The icy mud, the puny bud,
The frozen daffodils.
Let other poets gaily sing;
I do not like the signs of spring.

I do not like the foggy fall
That strips the maples bare;
The radiator's mating call,
The dank, rheumatic air;
I fear that taken all in all,
I do not like the foggy fall.

The winter sun, of course, is kind,
And summer's wind a saviour,
And I'll merrily sing of fall and spring
When they're on their good behaviour.
But otherwise I see no reason
To speak in praise of any season.

Ogden Nash

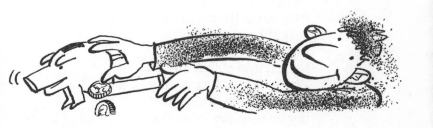

PENNIES FROM HEAVEN

I put 10p in my Piggy Bank
To save for a rainy day.
It rained the *very next morning!*
Three Cheers, Hip Hip Hooray!

Spike Milligan

DEATH OF A SNOWMAN

I was awake all night,
Big as a polar bear,
Strong and firm and white.
The tall black hat I wear
Was draped with ermine fur.
I felt so fit and well
Till the world began to stir
And the morning sun swell.
I was tired, began to yawn;
At noon in the humming sun
I caught a severe warm;
My nose began to run.
My hat grew black and fell,
Was followed by my grey head.
There was no funeral bell,
But by tea-time I was dead.

Vernon Scannell

WINTER MORNING

Winter is the king of showmen,
Turning tree stumps into snow men
And houses into birthday cakes
And spreading sugar over lakes.
Smooth and clean and frosty white,
The world looks good enough to bite.
That's the season to be young,
Catching snowflakes on your tongue.
Snow is snowy when it's snowing,
I'm sorry it's slushy when it's going.

Ogden Nash

THE SNOWMAN

Mother, while you were at the shops
and I was snoozing in my chair
I heard a tap at the window
saw a snowman standing there

He looked so cold and miserable
I almost could have cried
so I put the kettle on
and invited him inside

I made him a cup of cocoa
to warm the cockles of his nose
then he snuggled in front of the fire
for a cosy little doze

He lay there warm and smiling
softly counting sheep
I eavesdropped for a little while
then I too fell asleep

Seems he awoke and tiptoed out
exactly when I'm not too sure
it's a wonder you didn't see him
as you came in through the door

(oh, and by the way,
the kitten's made a puddle on the floor)

Roger McGough

182

IT'S SPRING, IT'S SPRING

It's spring, it's spring –

when everyone sits round a roaring fire
telling ghost stories!

It's spring, it's spring –

when everyone sneaks into everyone else's yard
and bashes up their snowman!

It's spring, it's spring –

when the last dead leaves fall from the trees
and Granny falls off your toboggan!

It's spring, it's spring –

when you'd give your right arm
for a steaming hot bowl of soup!

It's spring, it's spring –

when you'd give your right leg
not to be made to wash up after Christmas dinner!

It's spring, it's spring –

isn't it?

Kit Wright

WINDSHIELD WIPERS

Windshield wipers
Wipe away the rain,
Please bring the sunshine
Back again.

Windshield wipers
Clean our car,
The fields are green
And we're travelling far.

My father's coat is warm
My mother's lap is deep
Windshield wipers
Carry me to sleep.

And when I wake,
The sun will be
A golden home
Surrounding me;

But if that rain gets worse
Gets worse instead,
I want to sleep
Till I'm in bed.

Windshield wipers
Wipe away the rain,
Please bring the sunshine
Back again.

Dennis Lee

ECLIPSE

I looked the sun straight in the eye
He put on dark glasses

F. R. Scott

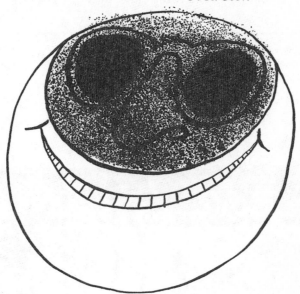

THE WIND AND THE MOON

Said the Wind to the Moon,
'I will blow you out;
   You stare
   In the air
   Like a ghost in a chair
Always looking what I am about.
I hate to be watched – I'll blow
       you out.'

George MacDonald

ALL THE TIME

If
we dug a hole
through the moon
we could have light
all the time.

The sun
would shine
through
at night.

Ivor Cutler

ROOMING HOUSE

The blind man draws his curtains for the night
and goes to bed, leaving a burning light

above the bathroom mirror. Through the wall,
he hears the deaf man walking down the hall

in his squeaky shoes to see if there's a light
under the blind man's door, and all is right.

Ted Kooser

THE AIR

The air was once about to die.

It cried: 'O help me, Lord on high;
I am distressed and feeling sick,
am getting sluggish, getting thick;
you always know a way, Papa:
send me abroad, or to a spa,
or buttermilk may cure and heal –
else to the devil I'll appeal!'

The Lord, perturbed by this affair,
invented 'sound massage for air.'

Since then the world is full of noise,
which thrivingly the air enjoys.

Christian Morgenstern

THE TWO ROOTS

A pair of pine roots, old and dark,
make conversation in the park.

The whispers where the top leaves grow
are echoed in the roots below.

An agèd squirrel sitting there
is knitting stockings for the pair.

The one says: squeak. The other: squawk.
That is enough for one day's talk.

Christian Morgenstern

THE HOUSE ON THE HILL

It was built years ago
by someone quite manic
and sends those who go there
away in blind panic.
They tell tales of horrors
that can injure or kill
designed by the madman
who lived on the hill.

> If you visit the House on the Hill for a dare
> remember my words . . .
>
> 'There are dangers. Beware!'

The piano's white teeth
when you plonk out a note
will bite off your fingers
then reach for your throat.
The living room curtains
– long, heavy and black –
will wrap you in cobwebs
if you're slow to step back.

> If you enter the House on the Hill for a dare
> remember my words . . .
>
> 'There are dangers. Beware!'

The 'fridge in the kitchen
has a self-closing door.
If it knocks you inside
then you're ice cubes . . . for sure.
The steps to the cellar
are littered with bones,
and up from the darkness
drift creakings and groans.

If you go to the House on the Hill for a dare
remember my words . . .

               'There are dangers. Beware!'

Turn on the hot tap
and the bathroom will flood
not with gallons of water
but litres of blood.
The rocking-chair's arms
can squeeze you to death;
a waste of time shouting
as you run . . . out . . . of . . . breath.

Don't say you weren't warned or told to take care
when you entered the House on the Hill . . .

               for a dare.

Wes Magee

EACH NIGHT FATHER FILLS ME WITH DREAD

Each night father fills me with dread
When he sits on the foot of my bed;
    I'd not mind that he speaks
    In gibbers and squeaks,
But for seventeen years he's been dead.

Edward Gorey

BUMP

Things that go 'bump' in the night
Should not really give one a fright.
It's the hole in each ear
That lets in the fear,
That, and the absence of light!

Spike Milligan

HANDSAW

HANDSAWWWWWWWWWWWWWWWWWW

Richard Lebovitz

NOTTING HILL POLKA

We've – had –
A Body in the house
    Since father passed away:
He took bad on
Saturday night an' he
    Went the following day.

Mum's – pulled –
The blinds all down
    An' bought some Sherry Wine,
An' we've put the tin
What the Arsenic's in
At the bottom of the Ser-pen-tine!

W. Bridges-Adam

THE MOON

The moon paints faces on the houses,
Gives them eyes and gives them mouthses
Paints a grin where there was none
And now that things of day are gone

He stretches shadows on the midden,
And jumps the cats from where they're hidden
He silvers puddles, gilds the cobbles
And makes my shadow twitch and hobble

And limp behind me through the park
The moon makes daydreams of the dark
And when you're walking past old statues
He makes them wink and then come at you.

If ever on moonlit nights I roam
I always wish that I'd stayed home.

Mike Harding

COLONEL FAZACKERLEY

Colonel Fazackerley Butterworth-Toast
Bought an old castle complete with a ghost,
But someone or other forgot to declare
To Colonel Fazack that the spectre was there.

On the very first evening, while waiting to dine,
The Colonel was taking a fine sherry wine,
When the ghost, with a furious flash and a flare,
Shot out of the chimney and shivered, 'Beware!'

Colonel Fazackerley put down his glass
And said, 'My dear fellow, that's really first class!
I just can't conceive how you do it at all.
I imagine you're going to a Fancy Dress Ball?'

At this, the dread ghost gave a withering cry.
Said the Colonel (his monocle firm in his eye),
'Now just how you do it I wish I could think.
Do sit down and tell me, and please have a drink.'

The ghost in his phosphorous cloak gave a roar
And floated about between ceiling and floor.
He walked through a wall and returned through a pane
And backed up the chimney and came down again.

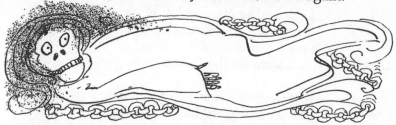

Said the Colonel, 'With laughter I'm feeling quite weak!'
(As trickles of merriment ran down his cheek).
'My house-warming party I hope you won't spurn.
You *must* say you'll come and you'll give us a turn!'

At this, the poor spectre – quite out of his wits –
Proceeded to shake himself almost to bits.
He rattled his chains and he clattered his bones
And he filled the whole castle with mumbles and moans.

But Colonel Fazackerley, just as before,
Was simply delighted and called out, 'Encore!'
At which the ghost vanished, his efforts in vain,
And never was seen at the castle again.

'Oh dear, what a pity!' said Colonel Fazack.
'I don't know his name, so I can't call him back.'
And then with a smile that was hard to define,
Colonel Fazackerley went in to dine.

Charles Causley

He thought he saw a Buffalo,
    Upon the chimney-piece:
He looked again, and found it was
    His Sister's Husband's Niece.
'Unless you leave this house,' he said,
    'I'll send for the Police!'

He thought he saw a Rattlesnake,
    That questioned him in Greek;
He looked again, and found it was
    The Middle of Next Week.
'The one thing I regret,' he said,
    'Is that it cannot speak!'

He thought he saw a Banker's Clerk
  Descending from a bus;
He looked again, and found it was
  A Hippopotamus.
'If this should stay to dine,' he said,
  'There won't be much for us!'

He thought he saw a Kangaroo
  That worked a coffee mill:
He looked again, and found it was
  A Vegetable Pill.
'Were I to swallow this,' he said,
  'I should be very ill!'

He thought he saw a Coach-and-four
  That stood beside his bed;
He looked again, and found it was
  A Bear without a Head;
'Poor thing,' he said, 'poor silly thing!
  It's waiting to be fed!'

He thought he saw an Albatross
  That fluttered round the Lamp;
He looked again, and found it was
  A Penny-Postage-Stamp.
'You'd best be getting home,' he said,
  'The nights are very damp!'

Lewis Carroll

WHO'S THAT

Who's that
stopping at
my door in the
dark, deep in the dead of the moonless night?

Who's
that in the quiet
blackness, darker than dark?

Who
turns the han-
dle of my door, who
turns the old brass hand-
le of
my door with never a sound, the handle
that always creaks and rattles and
squeaks but
now
turns
without a sound, slowly
slowly,
  slowly
    round?

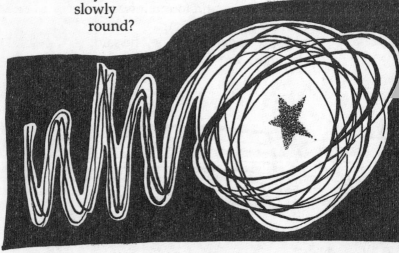

Who's that moving through the floor
as if it were a lake, an open door? Who
is it who passes through
what can never be passed through?
who passes through
the rocking-chair
without rocking it,
who passes through
the table without knocking it, who
walks out of the cupboard without unlocking it?
Who's that? Who plays with my toys
with no noise, no
noise?

Who's that? Who is it
silent and silver
as things in mirrors, who's
as slow as feathers,
shy as the shivers,
light as a fly?

Who's that who's that
as close as
close as a hug, a kiss –

Who's THIS?

James Kirkup

WELL, IT'S TODAY ALREADY

Well, it's today already.

I don't know how it got here,
but there's a funny echo in this room.   room

Martin Hall

THE TROUBLE WITH MY SISTER

My little sister was truly awful,
She was really shocking,
She put the budgie in the fridge
And slugs in Mummy's stocking.

She was really awful,
But it was a load of fun
When she stole old Uncle Wilbur's
Double-barrelled gun.

She aimed it at a pork pie
And blew it into bits,
She aimed it at a hamster
That was having fits.

She leapt up on the telly,
She pirouetted on the cat,
She gargled with some jelly
And spat in Grandad's hat.

She ran down the hallway,
She ran across the road,
She dug up lots of little worms
And caught a squirming toad.

She put them in a large pot
And she began to stir,
She added a pint of bat's blood
And some rabbit fur.

She leapt upon the Hoover,
Around the room she went,
Once she had a turned-up nose
But now her nose is bent.

I like my little sister,
There is really just one hitch,
I think my little sister
Has become a little witch.

Brian Patten

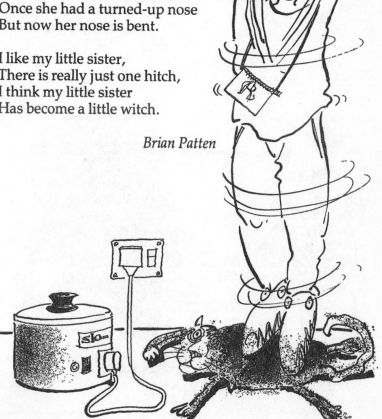

BEWARE

This cunning creature in its lair,
You'll find, is lurking everywhere.
There may be one (or even two).
It could be sitting next to you.
With staring eyes it's on the prowl.
It gives a sudden roar (or howl)
And, in a flash, to your dismay
It's leaping forward to its prey.
Beware each night this fearful danger –
The dreaded telly channel changer.

Max Fatchen

THE EXECUTION

On the night of the execution
a man at the door
mistook me for the coroner.
'Press,' I said.

But he didn't understand. He led me
into the wrong room
where the sheriff greeted me:
'You're late, Padre.'

'You're wrong,' I told him. 'I'm Press.'
'Yes, of course, Reverend Press.'
We went down the stairway.

'Ah, Mr. Ellis,' said the Deputy.
'Press!' I shouted. But he shoved me
through a black curtain.
The lights were so bright
I couldn't see the faces
of the men sitting
opposite. But, thank God, I thought
they can see me!

'Look!' I cried. 'Look at my face!
Doesn't anybody know me?'

Then a hood covered my head.
'Don't make it harder for us,' the hangman whispered.

Alden Nowlan

THE LOCH NESS MONSTER'S SONG

Sssnnnwhufffll?
Hnwhuffl hhnnwfl hnfl hfl?
Gdroblboblhobngbl gbl gl g g g g glbgl.
Drublhaflablhaflubhafgabhaflhafl fl fl –
gm grawwwww grf grawf awfgm graw gm.
Hovoplodok-doplodovok-plovodokot-doplodokosh?
Splgraw fok fok splgrafhatchgabrlgabrl fok splfok!
Zgra kra gka fok!
Grof grawff gahf?
Gombl mbl bl –
blm plm,
blm plm,
blm plm,
blp.

Edwin Morgan

O HERE IT IS! AND THERE IT IS!

O here it is! And there it is!
And no one knows whose share it is
Nor dares to stake a claim –
But we have seen it in the air
A fairy like a William Pear –
With but itself to blame.

A thug it is – and smug it is
And like a floating pug it is
Above the orchard trees
It has no right – no right at all
To soar above the orchard wall
With chilblains on its knees.

Mervyn Peake

SOME ONE

Some one came knocking
    At my wee, small door;
Some one came knocking,
    I'm sure – sure – sure;

I listened, I opened,
    I looked to left and right,
But nought there was a-stirring
    In the still dark night;

Only the busy beetle
    Tap-tapping in the wall,
Only from the forest
    The screech-owl's call,

Only the cricket whistling
    While the dewdrops fall,
So I know not who came knocking,
    At all, at all, at all.

Walter De La Mare

SO BIG!

The dinosaur, an ancient beast,
I'm told, was very large.
His eyes were big as billiard balls,
His stomach, a garage.
He had a huge and humping back,
A neck as long as Friday.
I'm glad he lived so long ago
And doesn't live in my day!

Max Fatchen

THE DINOSAURS ARE NOT ALL DEAD

The dinosaurs are not all dead.
I saw one raise its iron head
To watch me walking down the road
Beyond our house today.
Its jaws were dripping with a load
Of earth and grass that it had cropped.
It must have heard me where I stopped,
Snorted white steam my way,
And stretched its long neck out to see,
And chewed, and grinned quite amiably.

Charles Malam

ELEPHANT

It is quite unfair to be
obliged to be so large, so I suppose
you could call me discontented.

Think big, they said, when
I was a little elephant; they
wanted to get me used to it.

It was kind. But it doesn't help if,
inside, you are carefree in small ways,
fond of little amusements.

You are smaller than me, think
how conveniently near the flowers are,
how you can pat the cat by just

halfbending over. You can also
arrange teacups for dolls, play
marbles in the proper season.

I would give anything to be
able to do a tiny, airy, flitting
dance to show how very little a

thing happiness can be really.

Alan Brownjohn

ANT AND ELEPH-ANT

Said a tiny Ant
To the Elephant,
'Mind how you tread in this clearing!'

But alas! Cruel fate!
She was crushed by the weight
Of an Elephant, hard of hearing.

Spike Milligan

ANTEATER

Anteater, Anteater
Where have you been?
Aunt Liz took you walkies
And hasn't been seen.

Nor has Aunt Mary,
Aunt Flo or Aunt Di.
Anteater, Anteater
Why the gleam in your eye?

S. K. Werp

FRENCH VERSION

Tantemanger, Tantemanger
Comment allez-vous?
Tante Claire se promenait,
Et a disparu.

Aussi Tante Marie,
Tantes Simone et Lulu.
Tantemanger, Tantemanger,
Pourquoi souriez-vous?

Roger McGough

A CRUEL MAN A BEETLE CAUGHT

A cruel man a beetle caught,
And to the wall him pinned, oh!
Then said the beetle to the crowd,
'Though I'm stuck up I am not proud,'
And his soul went out of the window.

Anonymous

HOUSE FLIES

What makes
common house flies
trying
is
that they keep
multiflieing

Niels Mogens Bodecker

THE FLY

God in his wisdom made the fly
And then forgot to tell us why.

Ogden Nash

GIGL

a pigl
wigl
if
u
tigl

Arnold Spika

THE TERNS

Said the mother Tern
    to her baby Tern
Would you like a brother?
Said baby Tern
    to mother Tern
Yes
One good Tern deserves another.

Spike Milligan

THE TORTOISE AND THE HARE

Languid, lethargic, listless and slow,
The tortoise would dally, an image of sloth.
'Immobile', 'Stagnant', to the hare it was both.

'Enough of your insults, I seek satisfaction.
I'll run you a race and win by a fraction.'
Thus challenged the tortoise one afternoon.
'Right,' said the hare, 'and let it be soon.'

They decided they'd race right through the wood,
And the tortoise set off as fast as it could.
The hare followed at a leisurely pace
Quite confident that it could win the race.

The tortoise thought as it ambled along,
'I have never been faster, or quite so strong.'
The hare on the other hand was often inclined
To stop at the wayside and improve its mind.

It read a fable by Aesop deep in the wood,
Then of course it set off as fast as it could.
It decided it would put that fable aright
As it sped along with the speed of light.

Languid, lethargic, listless and slow
The tortoise ran fast as a tortoise could go.
Yet the hare having decided on saving face
Quite easily managed to win the race.

'I feel,' said the tortoise, 'that I have been deceived,
For fables are things I have always believed.
I would love to have won a race clearly designed
To point out a moral both old and refined.'

'Losing a race would not matter,' the hare said,
'For in speed Mother Nature placed me ahead.
Some fables are things you ought to contest,
Dear Tortoise, in mine, I'm afraid you've come last.'

Brian Patten

MR KARTOFFEL

Mr Kartoffel's a whimsical man;
He drinks his beer from a watering-can,
And for no good reason that I can see
He fills his pockets with china tea.
He parts his hair with a knife and fork
And takes his ducks for a Sunday walk.
Says he, 'If my wife and I should choose
To wear our stockings outside our shoes,
Plant tulip bulbs in the baby's pram
And eat tobacco instead of jam,
And fill the bath with cauliflowers,
That's nobody's business at all but ours.'

James Reeves

RHUBARB TED

I knew a funny little man
His name was Rhubarb Ted;
They called him that because he wore
Rhubarb on his head.

I'd grown so used to this strange sight,
The cause I did not seek;
But then one day to my surprise,
I saw he wore a leek.

I asked him if he'd please explain,
And let me know the reason;
He said, 'I'm wearing leek because
Rhubarb's out of season!'

Ann O'Connor

A NURSE MOTIVATED BY SPITE

A nurse motivated by spite
Tied her infantine charge to a kite;
   She launched it with ease
   On the afternoon breeze,
And watched till it flew out of sight.

Edward Gorey

A CERTAIN YOUNG MAN IT WAS NOTED

A certain young man, it was noted,
Went about in the heat thickly-coated;
  He said, 'You may scoff,
  But I shan't take it off;
Underneath I am horribly bloated.'

Edward Gorey

TWO FUNNY MEN

I know a man
Who's upside down,
And when he goes to bed
His head's not on the pillow, No!
His *feet* are there instead.

I know a man
Who's back to front,
The strangest man *I've* seen.
He can't tell where he's going
But he knows where he has been.

Spike Milligan

ANNA ELISE

Anna Elise, she jumped with surprise;
The surprise was so quick, it played her a trick;
The trick was so rare, she jumped in a chair;
The chair was so frail she jumped in a pail;
The pail was so wet, she jumped in a net;
The net was so small, she jumped on the ball;
The ball was so round, she jumped on the ground;
And ever since then she's been turning around.

Anonymous

CARELESS WILLIE

Willie, with a thirst for gore,
Nailed his sister to the door.
Mother said, with humour quaint:
'Now, Willie dear, don't scratch the paint.'

Anonymous

SIR SMASHAM UPPE

Good afternoon, Sir Smasham Uppe!
We're having tea: do take a cup!
Sugar and milk? Now let me see –
Two lumps, I think? . . . Good gracious me!
The silly thing slipped off your knee!
Pray don't apologize, old chap:
A very trivial mishap!
So clumsy of you? How absurd!
My dear Sir Smasham, not a word!
Now do sit down and have another,
And tell us all about your brother –
You know, the one who broke his head.
Is the poor fellow still in bed? –
A chair – allow me, sir! . . . Great Scott!
That was a nasty smash! Eh, what?
Oh, not at all: the chair was old –
Queen Anne, or so we have been told.
We've got at least a dozen more:
Just leave the pieces on the floor.
I want you to admire our view:
Come nearer to the window, do:
And look how beautiful . . . Tut, tut!
You didn't see that it was shut?
I hope you are not badly cut!
Not hurt? A fortunate escape!
Amazing! Not a single scrape!
And now, if you have finished tea,
I fancy you might like to see
A little thing or two I've got.
That china plate? Yes, worth a lot:
A beauty too . . . Ah, there it goes!
I trust it didn't hurt your toes?
Your elbow brushed it off the shelf?
Of course: I've done the same myself.

And now, my dear Sir Smasham – Oh,
You surely don't intend to go?
You must be off? Well, come again.
So glad you're fond of porcelain!

E. V. Rieu

BRIAN

Brian is a baddie,
As nasty as they come.
He terrifies his daddy
And mortifies his mum.

One morning in December
They took him to the zoo,
But Brian lost his temper
And kicked a kangaroo.

And then he fought a lion
Escaping from its pit.
It tried to swallow Brian
Till Brian swallowed it!

Yes, Brian is a devil,
A horrid little curse –
Unlike his brother Neville
Who's infinitely worse!

Doug Macleod

BRENDA BAKER

Brenda Baker, quite ill-bred,
Used to cuddle fish in bed.
Tuna, trout and conger-eels,
Salmon, sole and sometimes seals.
Barracuda, bream and bass,
She cuddled them, until – alas!
One unforgotten Friday night
She slept with two piranhas,
And, being rather impolite,
They ate her best pyjamas!

Doug Macleod

OLD HANK

For a lark,
For a prank,
Old Hank
Walked a plank.
These bubbles mark
    O
    O
    O
    O
    O
Where Hank sank.

Anonymous

PSYCHOLOGICAL PREDICTION

I think little Louie will turn out a crook. He
Puts on rubber gloves when stealing a cookie.

Virginia Brasier

DAINTY DOTTIE DEE

There's no one as immaculate
as dainty Dottie Dee,
who clearly is the cleanest
that a human being can be,
no sooner does she waken
than she hoses down her bed,
then hurries to the kitchen,
and disinfects the bread.

She spends the morning sweeping
every inch of every room,
when all the floors are spotless,
Dottie polishes the broom,
she mops the walls and ceilings,
she scrubs beneath the rug,
and should a bug meander by,
she tidies up that bug.

Dottie boils the phone and toaster,
Dotties rinses the shampoo,
she waxes the salami,
and she vacuums the stew,
she dusts the cheese and crackers,
and she sponges down the pie,
she lathers the spaghetti,
then hangs it up to dry.

Dottie scours the locks and keyholes,
and she soaps the bathroom scale,
she launders every light bulb,
she bathes the morning mail,
but her oddest habit ever
(and of this there's little doubt)
is washing all the garbage
before she throws it out.

Jack Prelutsky

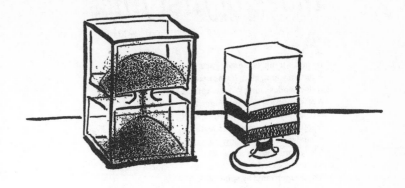

SKWERP EGGS

Have you ever seen
a skwerp?

Ever heard its plain-
tive cry? (skwerp! skwerp!)

Ever tasted a
skwerp egg?

Delicious. Give one
a try.

Fry gently in a
square pan

(why not a round one?
won't fit)

cut neatly into
four cubes

say grace, then eat
every bit (slurp! slurp!)

S. K. Werp

index of first lines

A

B

C

J

K

L

M

N

O

index of poets

acknowledgements

The editor and publishers gratefully acknowledge permission to reproduce the following copyright material:

Allan Ahlberg: 'I Did a Bad Thing Once', 'Picking Teams' and 'Supply Teacher' from *Please Mrs. Butler* by Allan Ahlberg (Kestrel Books 1983, London), pp. 16–17, 35, 38, copyright © 1983 by Allan Ahlberg. Reproduced by permission of Penguin Books Ltd. Michael Baldwin: 'The Truth About the Abominable Footprint'. Reprinted by permission of the author. George Barker: 'The Cheetah, my dearest' from *Runes and Rhymes and Tunes and Chimes*. Reprinted by permission of Faber & Faber Ltd. Hilaire Belloc: 'Jack and his pony, Tom', 'The Python', and 'The Scorpion' from *Cautionary Tales* by Hilaire Belloc. Reprinted by permission of Gerald Duckworth & Co. Ltd. Carey Blyton: 'Night Starvation' from *Bananas in Pyjamas*. Reprinted by permission of the author. Niels Mogens Bodecker: 'House Flies' from *Hurry Hurry Mary Dear! And Other Nonsense Poems*. Copyright © 1976 N.M. Bodecker. (A Margaret K. McElderry Book). Reprinted with the permission of Atheneum Publishers, Inc. and J.M. Dent & Sons Ltd. Keith Bosley: 'The Fastest Train in the World' from *And I Dance* by Keith Bosley is reproduced with the permission of Angus & Robertson (UK) Ltd. Virginia Brasier: 'Psychological Predictions' reprinted by permission; © 1942, 1970 The New Yorker Magazine, Inc. W. Bridges-Adams: 'Notting Hill Polka' from *To Charlotte While Shaving*. Reprinted by permission of A. D. Peters & Co. Ltd. Alan Brownjohn: 'Bear' and 'Elephant' from *Brownjohn's Beasts* by Alan Brownjohn. Reprinted by permission of Macmillan, London and Basingstoke. Paul Camp: 'A Boy's Best Friend' from *Hard Lines 2: New Poetry and Prose*. Reprinted by permission of Faber & Faber Ltd. Charles Causley: 'Colonel Fazackerley' from *Figgie Hobbin* (Macmillan). Reprinted by permission. William Cole: 'Lost Contact'. Copyright 1973 William Cole. Reprinted by permission of the author. John Collis: 'Job Satisfaction'. Reprinted by permission of the author. Billy Connolly: 'I'd Rather be a Sausage'. Reprinted by permission of the author. Wendy Cope: 'Kenneth' from *Uncollected Poems*. Reprinted by permission of the author. 'Reading Scheme' from *Making Cocoa for Kingsley Amis* by Wendy Cope. Reprinted by permission of Faber & Faber Ltd. Ivor Cutler: 'Jungle Tips' and 'All the Time'. Reprinted by permission of the author. Walter de la Mare: 'Someone'. Reprinted by permission of The Literary Trustees of Walter de la Mare and The Society of Authors as their representative. Jan Dean: 'The Rubber Plant Speaks'. Reprinted by permission of the author. Peter Dixon: 'Colour of My Dreams', 'Questions' and 'Teabags'. Reprinted by permission of the author. Carol Ann Duffy: 'Nursery Rhyme'. Reprinted by permission of the author. Caroline Emerson: 'The Ups and Downs of the Elevator Car' from the *Fontana Lions Book of Young Verse*. Reprinted by permission of Fontana Paperbacks. Gavin Ewart: 'Americans' from *All My Little Ones* (Anvil Press), 'A Lunatic's London', 'The Madness of a Headmistress' and 'Xmas for the Boys' from *The Collected Ewart 1933–1980* (Century Hutchinson Limited). Reprinted by permission of the author. Max Fatchen: 'Jump Over the Moon', 'Look Out' and 'So Big' from *Songs for My Dog and Other People* by Max Fatchen (Kestrel Books 1980, London), pp. 30, 57, 14, copyright © 1980 by Max Fatchen. 'Beware', 'Ears', 'Pussycat, Pussycat' and 'Windy' from *Wry Rhymes for Troublesome Times* by Max Fatchen (Kestrel Books 1983, London), pp. 35, 75, 21, 58, copyright © 1981 by Max Fatchen. Reproduced by permission of Penguin Books Ltd. Michael Flanders: 'The Walrus' from *The Land of Utter Nonsense* by Colin West. Reprinted by permission of Arrow Publications. Roy Fuller: 'Advice to Children' from *Have You Seen Grandpa Lately?* Reprinted by permission of the author. Edward Gorey: 'A certain young man it was noted', 'Each night father fills me with dread', 'A lady born under a curse', and 'A nurse motivated by spite' from *The Listing Attic*, copyright © 1954 by Edward Gorey. Reprinted by permission of Deborah Rogers Ltd. and Candida Donadio & Associates, Inc. Mick Gowar: 'Christmas Thank You's' from *Swings and Roundabouts*. Reprinted by permission of Collins Publishers. Harry Graham: 'Quiet Fun' from *Ruthless Rhymes for Heartless Homes*. Reprinted by permission of Edward Arnold (Publishers) Ltd. Robert Graves: 'The Hero' from *Collected Poems 1975*. Reprinted by permission of the author. Mike Griffin: 'Oh To Be'. Reprinted by permission of the author. Mike Harding: 'Advice to Grownups and Other Animals', 'The Moon', 'My Uncle Fudge Told Lies' and 'The Revolt of the Lamp Posts' from *Up the Boo Aye, Shooting Pookakies*. First published by Savoy Books in 1980. Reprinted by permission of Moonraker Productions Ltd. Gregory Harrison: 'Distracted the mother said to her boy' from *Nine O'Clock Bell*. Reprinted by permission of the author. John Hegley: 'Contact Lenses', 'Grandad's Glasses', 'My Glasses' and 'Children with Adults' from *Visions of the Bone Idol*. Reprinted by permission of the author. Adrian Henri: 'Conversations on a Garden Wall' and 'Marigolds', copyright © 1986 by Adrian Henri. Used by permission of Deborah Rogers Ltd. Russell Hoban: 'The Friendly Cinnamon Bun'. Reprinted by permission of David Higham Associates Ltd. Sidney Hoddes: 'Mashed Potato/ Love Poem'. Reprinted by permission of the author. Martin Honeysett: 'When There's a Fire in the Jungle' from *What a Lot of Nonsense!* edited by John Foster. Reprinted by permission of Robert Royce Ltd. Ted Hughes: 'Grandma' from *Meet My Folks* by Ted Hughes. Reprinted by permission of Faber & Faber Ltd. and Olwyn Hughes. Mark Jones: 'Too Fast to Live, Too Young to Work' from *Hard Lines 2: New Poetry and Prose*. Reprinted by permission of Faber & Faber Ltd. Terry Jones: 'Frank Carew Macgraw'. Reprinted by permission of the author. James Kirkup: 'Who's That'. Reprinted by permission of the author. Ted Kooser: 'Rooming House'

Books (A Division of William Morrow & Co.). Monty Python: 'All Things Dull and Ugly' from *Monty Python's Life of Brian* and 'Horace Poem' from *Monty Python's Big Red Book* by Michael Palin, Eric Idle, Graham Chapman, Terry Jones, John Cleese and Terry Gilliam. Reprinted by permission of Methuen London. James Reeves: 'Mr Kartoffel' from *James Reeves: The Complete Poems* by James Reeves, © James Reeves Estate. Reprinted by permission of The James Reeves Estate. John Rice: 'On Some Other Planet' from *Rockets and Quasars* by John Rice. Reprinted by permission of the author. Michael Rosen: 'Dear Maureen' from *Wouldn't You Like to Know* (1977) and 'This is the Hand' from *Mind Your Own Business* (1974) by Michael Rosen. Reprinted by permission of Andre Deutsch Ltd. 'The Hardest Thing To Do In The World' from *You Tell Me* by Roger McGough and Michael Rosen (Kestrel Books 1979, London), p. 38, Michael Rosen poems copyright © 1979 by Michael Rosen, collection copyright © 1979 by Penguin Books Ltd. Reproduced by permission of Penguin Books Ltd. Willie Russell: 'I Wish I Was Our Sammy' from *Blood Brothers* by Willie Russell. Reprinted by permission of Methuen London. Maurice Sagoff: 'Robinson Crusoe' from *Shrinklits*. Reprinted by permission of Workman Publishing Company (New York). Vernon Scannell: 'Death of a Snowman' and 'Intelligence Test'. Reprinted by permission of the author. F.R. Scott: 'Eclipse' from *Collected Poems* by F.R. Scott. Used by permission of The Canadian Publishers, McClelland and Stewart Limited, Toronto. Ian Serraillier: 'The Tickle Rhyme' from *The Monster Horse* by Ian Serraillier, © 1950 Ian Serraillier and Oxford University Press. Reprinted by permission of the author. Shel Silverstein: 'Anchored', 'Batty' and 'Whatif' from *A Light in the Attic* by Shel Silverstein. Copyright © 1981 by Snake Eye Music, Inc. Reprinted by permission of Harper & Row, Publishers, Inc. and Jonathan Cape Ltd. Stevie Smith: 'Our Doggy' from *The Collected Poems of Stevie Smith*. Copyright © 1972 by Stevie Smith. Reprinted by permission of James MacGibbon, the executor. Arnold Spilka: 'Gigl' from *A Lion I Can Do Without* by Arnold Spilka (Walck), 1964 copyright. Permission granted by the author. Bernard Stone: 'The Charge of the Mouse Brigade'. Reprinted by permission of Andersen Press Ltd. Robert Sund: 'The Hawk' from *Bunch Grass* by Robert Sund. Reprinted by permission of the University of Washington Press. Matthew Sweeney: 'Grandpa's Monkeys'. Reprinted by permission of the author. Colleen Thibaudeau: 'as big as'. Reprinted by permisson of the author. Colin West: 'My Obnoxious Brother', 'Norman Norton's Nostrils' and 'When Rover Passed Over' from *Not to be Taken Seriously*. Reprinted by permission of Century Hutchinson Publishing Group Ltd. Roger Woddis: 'Fish Toes'. Reprinted by permission of the author. David Wood: 'I've Got My Head Stuck', 'I Saw You' and 'Marvo'. Copyright © David Wood 1986, reproduced by permission of Curtis Brown Ltd., London. Peggy Wood: 'My Aunt'. Reprinted by permission of Punch (London). Kit Wright: 'Give Up Slimming Mum', 'If You're No Good at Cooking' and 'My Dad, Your Dad' from *Rabbiting On* by Kit Wright. Reprinted by permission of Fontana Paperbacks. 'Greedyguts', 'It's Spring' and 'Laurie and Dorrie' from *Hot Dog and Other Poems* by Kit Wright (Kestrel Books 1981, London), pp. 32–33, 15, 66–67, copyright © 1981 by Kit Wright. Reproduced by permission of Penguin Books Ltd. Denis Doyle: 'Shirley Said'. Reprinted by permission of the author.

The editor and publishers would particularly like to thank Nan Froman for her work in obtaining permissions for this book. While every effort has been made to obtain permission, there may still be cases in which we have failed to trace a copyright holder, and we would like to apologize for any apparent negligence.